Selected Early Poems
Lev Loseff

*Translated
with notes and introduction
by Henry W. Pickford*

SPUYTEN DUYVIL

New York City

copyright ©2014 Lev Loseff
Translation copyright ©2014 Henry W. Pickford
ISBN 978-0-923389-97-0

A Kayden grant from the University of Colorado,
Boulder, partially underwrote the production costs
of this book.

Library of Congress
Cataloging-in-Publication Data

Losev, Lev, 1937-2009, author.
  [Poems. Selections. English. 2013]
  Selected early poems / Lev Loseff ; translated with
notes and introduction by Henry W. Pickford.
    pages ; cm
  ISBN 978-0-923389-97-0
  I. Pickford, Henry W., translator, writer of added
commentary. II. Title.
  PG3549.L58A2 2013
  891.71'44--dc23
                2013005705

Lev Loseff, his wife Nina, their two children Marie and Dimitry, with Joseph Brodsky on television.
Drawing by Vladimir Ufliand, 1989.

Portrait of Lev Loseff by Joseph Brodsky

Introduction

Nobody knew literature and history better than these people, nobody could write in Russian better than they, nobody despised our times more profoundly. For these characters civilization meant more than daily bread and a nightly hug. This wasn't, as it might seem, another lost generation. This was the only generation of Russians that had found itself, for whom Giotto and Mandelstam were more imperative than their own personal destinies. Poorly dressed but somehow still elegant, shuffled by the dumb hands of their immediate masters, running like rabbits from the ubiquitous state hounds and the even more ubiquitous foxes, broken, growing old, they still retained their love for the non-existent (or existing only in their balding heads) thing called 'civilization.' Hopelessly cut off from the rest of the world, they thought that at least that world was like themselves; now they know that it is like others, only better dressed. As I write this, I close my eyes and almost see them standing in their dilapidated kitchens, holding glasses in their hands, with ironic grimaces across their faces. "There, there ..." They grin. "*Liberté, Egalité, Fraternité* ... Why does nobody add Culture?"[1]

With these words the Nobel laureate Joseph Brodsky describes his generation of poets, whose identity, as he implied in the organizing trope of his elegiac memoir, amounted to "less than one": less than Russian since their passports bore the appellation "Jew" under "nationality" and having less than a career since they belonged to the marginalized class of intellectuals rather than to the party; if they were lucky enough to wash up in Vienna or Jerusalem or Brooklyn or Ann Arbor on the Third Wave of emigration, they were once again diminished, strangers in a strange land. A series of dislocations, accompanied by what Mandelstam called "the word as culture" and

---

1 Joseph Brodsky, "Less Than One," in his *Less Than One: Selected Essays* (New York: Farrar, Straus, Giroux, 1986), 29–30.

likened to a funeral ship conveying one's prized possessions to the afterlife. Displaced, shifted out of sync with so much of what reflects and reinforces one's sense of self, Brodsky declared, "Precisely in emigration I remained tête-à-tête with my language."[2] Philology preserves a particular kind of intimacy, of being at home in one's language when one's home has been lost.

Lev Lifshits was born on June 15, 1937, into an illustrious literary family headed by his father Vladimir, a well-known children's writer and poet. When Lev became editor at the renowned children's magazine *Kostyór* [*Campfire*],[3] his father anticipated that Lifshits *père et fils* would cause confusion and demanded that his son take a pseudonym. Lev responded by telling him to think up a name himself, and thus he acquired the name "Losev," which he anglicized to "Loseff" after emigrating to the United States with his wife Nina and their two children in 1976.[4]

In the United States Loseff worked as a typesetter and proofreader at the Ardis publishing house, earned a Ph.D. in Slavic languages and literatures from the University of Michigan, and taught Russian literature at Dartmouth College. It is perhaps not surprising that the twice-pseudonymed Loseff's first book of scholarship was devoted to the poetics of Aesopian language in Russian literature under the Soviets.[5]

While studying philology at Leningrad State University in the late 1950s, Loseff became a member of what came to be called the "philological school." The group of literary and cultural artists drew their inspiration chiefly from two early twentieth-century avant-garde movements closely associated with Russian Formalism. The

---

[2] Quoted in Sergey Gandlevskii, "Literatura^2 (literature v kvadrate): Mrachnaia veselost' L'va Loseva." *Znamia* 7 (July 1996): 198.

[3] Loseff recounted his experiences as a working Soviet writer and editor in essays and reviews that are collected in his *Zakrytii raspredelitel'* (Ann Arbor: Ardis, 1984) and in the poem "I used to work for *Campfire*. In that dreary place…," collected here.

[4] "Lifshits," however, anagrammatically accompanies several of Losev's poems, for instance, "Instructions to a Heraldic Illustrator," and is conjured in the first two lines of the second stanza of "In Memory of Lithuania."

[5] Lev Loseff, *On the Beneficence of Censorship: Aesopian Language in Modern Russian Literature* (Munich: Sagner Verlag, 1984).

Futurists (Velimir Khlebnikov, Vladimir Mayakovskii, David Burliuk, Kazimir Malevich, Aleksei Kruchenykh) understood themselves as hypermodernists who deconstructed and reconstructed the fundamental elements of language and the visual arts. The group OBERIU (Association of Real Art, founded in 1928 by Daniil Kharms, Aleksandr Vvedensky, and Nikolai Zabolotsky) was renowned for defamiliarizing everyday life by means of impromptu performance art, nonsensical verse, and dramaturgical poetics anticipating the theater of the absurd. In a later interview Loseff acknowledged that in the mid-1950s "most probably the influence of Zabolotsky and the Oberiu people was immense. ... There was a period during which I simply was studying them incessantly, digging up their texts, copying them, passing them around, and they somehow got into my blood."[6]

The founding members of the philological school were Mikhail Krasil'nikov and Iurii Mikhailov; not unlike the Situationists in Paris, they staged "Futurist demonstrations." In a memoir Loseff recounts one of their exploits:

> On December 1, 1951, several eighteen-year-old freshmen—Eduard Kondratov, Mikhail Krasil'nikov, Iurii Mikhailov, and two or three others—came to the university wearing boots and peasant shirts and, sitting on the floor in a circle during the break between lectures, ate kvass soup from a common bowl with wooden spoons, reciting poems of Khlebnikov that were suitable to the occasion and, as it were, realizing the Khlebnikovian pan-Slavic utopia.[7]

For these and similar antics Krasil'nikov and Mikhailov were suspended from the university and sent to work in factories for eighteen months. When Loseff and his friends Sergei Kulle, Aleksandr and Eduard Kondratov, Leonid Vinogradov, Mikhail Eremin, and Vladimir Ufliand enrolled at the university in 1954, they joined the group, taking autumn dips in the Neva River amid the drifting ice floes and staging their own alcohol-enabled Futurist "happenings":

---

[6] "Poet est' peregnoi. Beseda so L'vom Losevym," in *Zapechatlennye golosa: Parizhskie besedy s russkimi pisateliami i poetami*, ed. Vitalii Amurskii (Moscow: "MIK," 1998), 69.

[7] Lev Losev, "Tulupy my," in *Meandr* (Moscow: Novoe izdatel'stvo, 2010), 280.

> With Vinogradov and Eremin we were walking on Nevsky Prospect in the evening. It was crowded with people hurrying along on account of the frost. I said: "It would be nice to lie down for a bit." "It would be," said my companions and began to lie down. We laid on our backs on the sidewalk at the entrance of the former Masonic lodge building, where the editorial office of the journal *Neva* was later housed. As usual, the passersby did not know how to react. Several stopped and with respectful concern asked what was going on. We answered in a friendly manner that we were resting. This simple answer suddenly caused their ordinary faces to reflect torturous mental effort that seemed literally intolerable for the average Soviet passerby, and the people hastened to leave. We looked at the stars, normally not visible above Nevsky Prospect, and said something befitting the study of the stars: about Kant's moral imperative and, a topic fashionable at the time, about Fyodor Mikhailovich [Dostoevsky's] views on the balance of the Kantian antinomies.[8]

The combination of an absurdist, nonconformist attitude with a profound knowledge of Russian culture was a defining characteristic of the philological school.[9] Another characteristic was the near absolute significance accorded to intoxication. Loseff writes:

> Everything good in me I owe to vodka. Vodka was the catalyst of my spiritual emancipation; it opened doors into interesting undergrounds of the subconscious and at the same time trained me not to be afraid—of people, of authorities.
> It's quite remarkable that with such an intensive fondness for vodka only one or two of our group really became drunkards. We damaged our health, not to mention our careers, but that is another matter, an altogether small price to pay for freedom, for understanding, for wonderful poems.[10]

The deflationary allusion to Gorky's famous dictum "everything good in

---

8 Ibid., 282. Cf. also Loseff's remembrance of Ufliand: "Zhivoe teplo," in *Meandr*, 352–359.

9 See "*Filologicheskaia shkola.*" *Teksty: Vospominaniia. Bibliografiia*, ed. Viktor Kulle and Vladimir Ufliand (Moscow: "Letnii sad," 2006).

10 *Meandr*, 282.

me I owe to books," the more delicate nods to Huxley and Dostoevsky, and the intertwining of aesthetic, psychological, and political notions of liberation within Loseff's *apologia pro vino suo* could serve as interlinear notes to several poems in this collection, including the first cycle, "In Memory of Vodka."

In the preface to his first collection of poems, *The Wondrous Raid*, Loseff recounts that although as a young man he had written children's verse and plays for the puppet theater, it was only in 1974, at the age of thirty-seven (the age at which Pushkin died in a duel), that he started to write poetry; this was in part because his literary friends had ceased writing or were writing less, and in part it was a result of the careful and sustained self-examination following a heart attack he had suffered at the age of thirty-three.[11] Such attentive observation can be discerned in even the most ironic and self-deprecating of his poems collected here and characterizes his entire oeuvre. By his untimely death in 2009, Loseff had published six books of verse; a seventh appeared posthumously.

Loseff's profound and playful erudition has elicited various claims of influence and filiation. The poet himself told an interviewer that his influences were completely eclectic, naming among classical Russian writers Nikolai Nekrasov, Aleksei Tolstoy, and Afanasy Fet, and among Soviet writers Boris Slutsky, Leonid Martynov, and Dmitry Bykov.[12] With respect to his theme of childhood modulated by mordant wit, he has been likened to Kornei Chukovsky and Sasha Cherny.[13] In an important foreword to Loseff's poetic debut in the émigré journal *Ekho,* Brodsky wrote:

> The poems of A. [sic] Losev are a remarkable event of our native literature, for they open in it a page hitherto not contemplated.

---

11 Several poems in the present collection allude to Loseff's illness, including the third section of "Amphibronchic Night," "Pronouns," and especially "Midway in the journey of my earthly life...."

12 Responses to questions posed by the editor of "Okna," the literary supplement to the journal *Vesti,* February 2004, reprinted in M. Gronas and B. Scherr (eds.), *Лифшиц/Лосев/Loseff/левлосев* (Moscow: Novoe literaturnoe obozrenie, forthcoming).

13 Artem Skvortsov, "Tragedia pod maskoj ironii," *Voprosy literatury* 5 (2009): 32–43.

> To some degree or other, Russian poetry (especially poetry of
> the second half of the twentieth century) is always the poetry of
> extremes: extreme tragedy, extreme depression, extreme piety,
> extreme categoricalness, extreme irony, extreme esotericism,
> extreme self-destructive cynicism. A. Losev is a restrained poet,
> extremely restrained. Without doubt, in the works of any author
> chosen according to these definitions, one finds individual
> poems and even entire cycles marked by a disposition close to
> Losev's; however, it is always an interlude, the stopping place
> of a comic or tragic actor. Losev's restraint is a system, a system
> as much psychological as stylistic. The traditional character
> of his stanzas is itself a tribute to this restraint, for tradition
> is often only a noble name for a mask. Behind Losev's mask
> hides a lyrical hero of a new type in Russian poetry, not so
> much more complicated than the authors mentioned above, but
> rather having totally absorbed the complete palette of attitudes
> demonstrated by these authors. "Any powerful new poet," said
> the late poet T.S. Eliot, "changes the perspective of poetry."
> Possibly that is a little too broad a declaration; but it is without
> doubt that the verse of Losev will help the reader to understand
> better the perspective of Losev's contemporaries. "Who is he
> like?" is the usual question asked by a reader when encountering
> an unknown poet. *Like no one else*, I would like to answer; but
> the more I reread these poems, about whose existence I knew
> nothing at all for twenty years, the more often comes to my mind
> one of the most remarkable poets of the Petersburg Pleiade—
> Prince Pyotr Andreevich Vyazemsky. That restraint, that subdued
> tone, that dignity. Who could have guessed that in the fifties
> and sixties of our own century there would unfold on the banks
> of the Neva a poetic drama that had premiered a half century
> earlier?[14]

Brodsky's preface was reprinted together with a selection of Loseff's poems in an émigré anthology, one of whose editors printed a rejoinder to Brodsky, placing Loseff instead in the tradition of "bureaucrat (pardon!) poets," such as Fyodor Tyutchev or Innokenty Annensky, by virtue of his restraint and "character of a school teacher."[15] With this description we come close to another recognized type, the *poeta*

---

14 Brodsky, "O stikhax A. Loseva," *Ekho* 4 (1979): 65–66.

15 Konstantin K. Kuzminsky, in K. Kuzminsky and G. Kovalev (eds.), *The Blue Lagoon Anthology of Modern Russian Poetry,* vol. 2B (Newtonville, MA: Oriental Research Partners, 1986), 342–343.

doctus, or scholar-poet. Loseff's allusively intimate knowledge of Russian literature in its entirety as well as his facility with English, French, and German as evidenced by the multilingual puns that percolate through his verse suffice to earn him that laurel wreath. The English critic Gerald Smith has proposed the turn-of-century émigré poets Vladislav Khodasevich and Georgy Ivanov as predecessors by virtue of their technical proficiency and melancholy, almost elegiac, irony.[16] Other critics have suggested other influences and predecessors, each one highlighting certain contours of Loseff's verse while failing to mention significant differences, whereas perhaps one should speak not of the poet or author, but rather of his use of personae, masks, and *skaz* techniques—not an improper métier for a *poeta doctus*.[17]

Similarly, several critics succumb to the temptation of first developing a consistent portrait of the lyrical hero in several of Loseff's poems—usually that of the inebriated, ironic, coldly dispassionate émigré writer who is as likely to allude subtly to Pushkin as he is to cast caustic and vulgar epithets upon himself and others—and then identifying Loseff's most frequent lyric persona with the author himself. There is, of course, some independent evidence for suggesting some similarities between the person and the persona, such as Loseff's praise for vodka in his memoirs and its mention in several of his poems. Moreover, many poems manifest a clear-eyed existentialist self-reliance, accompanied at most with faint gestures of metaphysical or theological longing.[18] Similarly, when asked by an interviewer which of the three funeral services for Brodsky he found most moving, Loseff answered laconically: "I did not experience

---

16 Gerald S. Smith, "Flight of the Angels: The Poetry of Lev Loseff," *Slavic Review* 47, no. 1 (1988): 76–88.

17 Loseff speaks of masks in the meta-poems "An Interpretation of Tselkov" and "A poet is compost…"; his use of *skaz* is shown in poems such as "A Cat's Lament," "An onion in bandy slices…," and "Letter to the Old Country."

18 The unironical intimations of spirituality in Loseff's poetry have gone largely unnoticed by critics who fasten onto the depravity and uncouthness of some of his poems' subject matter or his lyrical persona and overlook that Loseff thereby is often condemning Soviet culture. Poems that gesture toward a higher spirituality include "I know, the Mongol yoke, the years of famine…," "Stanzas," and several lyrics from the cycle "Captions to Pictures Seen in Childhood."

any positive emotions from any of these organized events."[19] But in that same conversation Loseff cautions his interviewer against a fallacious identification by critics of Brodsky's lyrical hero with the author himself, and the same warning could certainly apply to Loseff and his work.[20] Thus, I would suggest that critics who find Loseff's verse uncentered or his lyrical hero to be tragic or melancholic or unfeeling or largely absent reexamine the assumption that his poetry is in some straightforward sense confessional before attributing such qualities to Loseff's own personality.[21] The relationship between psychology and poetics in the case of Loseff is more indirect, inflectional.

In an interview Loseff the *poeta doctus* notes the etymological relations between "*tkan*'" ("cloth") and "*tekst*" ("text"), which both derive from the Latin verb "*texere,*" "to weave," concluding: "All of us in some sense or other are weaving the text of our life."[22] Interwoven into the very fabric of Loseff's life is, however, the experience of frequent dislocations on the one hand and, on the other, the creative, fictional, even Aesopian nature of parts of that life as text. Psychology, history, and stylistics meet in Loseff's poetry in the Russian Formalist notion of "*sdvig*": "shift," "displacement," or "dislocation." Viktor Shklovsky adopted the concept and applied it to a variety of levels of literary analysis (syntactic, semantic, aesthetic, literary-historical) as one device by which a literary text achieves *ostranenie* or "defamiliarization," the effect of making reality strange or new by virtue of the text's *faktura*, its perceptible "texture," constructedness (materiality), or artistic "density."[23]

---

19 Valentina Polukhina, "Beseda s L'vom Losevym," *Zvezda* 1 (2005): 159–170, here p. 167.

20 Ibid., 166.

21 See, for instance, the following articles: Sergei Gandlevskii, "Literatura² (literatura v kvadrate): Mrachnaia veselost' L'va Loseva," *Zvezda* 7 (1996): 196–199; Artem Skvortsov, "Tragediia pod maskoj ironii," *Voprosy literatury* 5 (2009): 32–43; Andrei Ar'ev, "Nechuvstvitel'nyi," *Zvezda* 6 (2007): 134–139; the most intriguing interpretation along these lines is the review of Loseff's collected verse by Dmitrii Bykov, "Vokrug otsutstvia," *Novyi mir* 8 (2001): 190–192.

22 Polukhina, "Beseda," op. cit., 169. Cf. the poem "Cloth," collected here.

23 An excellent introduction to these concepts remains Victor Ehrlich, *Russian Formalism: History – Doctrine,* 2d ed. (The Hague: Mouton,1965).

The density of the text's weave, to remain with Loseff's chosen image, is determined by its shifts, displacements, such that the text constitutes a new experience or perception of reality. In his somber reflections on exile, Edward Said writes:

> Much of the exile's life is taken up with compensating for the disorienting loss by creating a new world to rule. It is not surprising that so many exiles seem to be novelists, chess players, political activists, and intellectuals. Each of these occupations requires a minimal investment in objects and places a great premium on mobility and skill. The exile's new world, logically enough, is unnatural and its unreality resembles fiction.[24]

My suggestion is that in Loseff, too, we can detect the impulse to create a new world, but that Loseff does *not* make that world or its chief inhabitant—his lyrical hero—a consistent, coherent, solid *substance*, liable to the claim of unreality and "fictionality" in the sense Said uses the term. Instead, Loseff's creations are decidedly *acts of displacement* in the Formalist sense: shifts in perspective, syntax, semantics that "lay bare the device," to use another Formalist slogan, of word- and life-weaving in the context of exile. The poems are neither a flight into fiction or literariness as such nor a diminution of the literary in favor of confessional authenticity; rather, *sdvig* as poetic form in Loseff's verse amounts to the assertion of the literariness of one's self-understanding, of one's attitude towards one's experience, mediated through Russian literary culture. In some extreme cases, one can shift oneself, perhaps only infinitesimally, from being the object of historical experience to becoming a kind of subject again by creating displacements of literary exuberance and brilliance. In his "new world to rule" Loseff has tweaked the rules to produce absurdist pleasure just as he did twenty years

---

[24] Edward Said, "Reflections on Exile," in his *Reflections on Exile and Other Essays* (Cambridge, MA: Harvard University Press, 2000), 181. Cf. Brodsky: "It started out as an ordinary accumulation of knowledge but soon became our most important occupation, to which everything could be sacrificed. Books became the first and only reality, whereas reality itself was regarded as either nonsense or nuisance. Compared to others, we were ostensibly flunking or faking our lives. But come to think of it, existence which ignores the standards professed in literature is inferior and unworthy of effort. So we thought, and I think we were right" (*Less Than One*, 28).

previously with his now displaced comrades of the philological school, though perhaps the pleasure is now tinged as well with the melancholic awareness that that school too has become "less than one."

There is a melancholic irony as well for the translator of Loseff, for the poet denied the possibility of successful translations of Russian poetry into English:

> Poetry is untranslatable. For more than a quarter century I've been teaching foreigners Russian literature, including poetry, and I know the great work that is required to explain even approximately how the poems of Pushkin or Akhmatova are so charming and fascinating for Russians. Moreover, the languages, Russian and English, are in a different condition. Russian more easily adapts foreign linguistic and poetic forms—syntax, stanzaic structures. Even more important, Russian is characterized by a more blurred semantics; it allows more ambiguity and multiple meanings. English is more stringent with referentiality: *A* indicates *B*, and if it doesn't indicate [anything], then the result is nonsense. Therefore, it's possible to schlep something to some degree from English into Russian, but not in the reverse direction. It's like a spigot that's made to allow passage in only one direction, and even then only reluctantly.²⁵

The specific untranslatability of Loseff's poems is due to their formal and semantic texture, their *faktura*. Among his contemporaries Loseff arguably deploys the most diverse array of metrical and rhyme schemes, drawing with ease on classical Russian poetry's tradition of syllabo-tonic metrical forms. Yet, even when working in the most popular metrical form in the Russian classical tradition, iambic tetrameter, Loseff adds complexity, as in "The Last Romance," where he varies the rhyme scheme in the concluding two stanzas, or in "The Regiment of Eros," where the concluding lines of the first three stanzas are halved into hemistichs.

---

25 Response to questions posed by the editor of "Okna," February 2004, reprinted in M. Gronas and B. Scherr (eds.), *Лифшиц/Лосев/Loseff/левлосев* (Moscow: Novoe literaturnoe obozrenie, forthcoming). Loseff continues: "A talented person, Gerald Smith (until recently he was chair of the Slavic department at Oxford) translated a few dozen of my poems into English and is preparing to publish a small book of them, but, from my point of view, they will be his texts, not mine (well, maybe one could say 'from' or 'following' mine)." Gerald Smith's literary translations of selected poems from Loseff's entire oeuvre have now appeared under the title *As I Said* (London: Arc Publications, 2012).

Loseff also works in other metrical schemes, such as ternary meters (e.g., anapests in "The Wondrous Raid," "Departure," and "The house is filled with warmth…"; dactyls in "In Memory of Lithuania"; amphibrachs in "We'd long ago grown deaf to nocturnal sounds…"), often combining different meters into his own polymetrical forms, and he uses stanzas of widely varying lengths and intricate rhyme schemes, as in the poems of the cycle "The Extended Day." A tour de force is his use of Dante's *terza rima* in "Midway in the journey of my earthly life… ." In "The Petrograd Side," the unrhymed iambic pentameter lines of the first two stanzas (themselves of varying numbers of lines) resolve, as it were, into a rhythm and rhyme form weaving together the last two stanzas, just as the poem describes the resumption of the way of the world. And in "A poet is compost…" the rhythm in the final two stanzas shifts from that of the first two, in which iambic tetrameter dominates, to a freer iambic trimeter, as though the poem's lines were decomposing. Loseff's astounding virtuosity flashes in his widely creative rhymes at the lexical level as well, often incorporating multilingual rhymes, [26] enjambment across a single word, [27] or paronomasia.[28] Loseff also experiments with nonclassical verse forms, for instance, concrete poetry, most obviously in poems such as "An onion in bandy slices…," "Instructions to the Heraldic Illustrator," and "Cloth." And in "M" the typography mimics the crenellations of the Kremlin's wall as well as the neon sign for the metro and the abbreviation for "Moscow." Loseff also occasionally experiments

---

26 For example: "на уме"/ "jamais" and "повымер"/ "immer" in "In Memory of Lithuania"; "о них же" / "Ницше" in "In a Park by the Rhine"; "Вермеер" / "вернее" and "memento ли mori?" / "море" in "In an Amsterdam Gallery"; "ни кола"/ "Nicolas" in "Verses on the Novel"; "à la gitane?" / "но как же там" in "Pushkin Historical Sites"; "table d'hôte" / "анекдот" in "The house is filled with warmth…"

27 For example: "дерев –" / "одурев" in "In a Park by the Rhine"; "бля –" / "скобля" in "Midway in the journey of my earthly life…"; "заря –" / "заря" in "3 Roubles"; "телодвиже –" / "Ж" in "Twelve Colleges." On Loseff's wordplay, see Liudmila Zubov, *Iazyki sovremennoi poezii* (Moscow: Novoe literaturnoe obozrenie, 2010).

28 For example: "Лиф поправляет лениво рыбачка. / Shit-c на песке оставляет собачка." (from "In Memory of Lithuania"), in which the first words of the two lines combine to form a pun of the author's original surname, and the word "лениво" suggests his first name.

with pure accentual verse ("Phaedra") and its more restricted form, the Russian *dólnik* (for instance, in "In an Amsterdam Gallery" and "In the Norman Hole," both from the cycle "The Journey," and in "PBG," "Cloth," and "Photography Lesson 1"), as well as with what some scholars might call free verse ("Dream"), both relatively rare verse forms in classical syllabo-tonic Russian poetry.[29]

The intricacies of the original verse are manifold, as the textual displacements occur on virtually every level of the text's *faktura*. For instance, Loseff explained how he wrote "The Regiment of Eros" this way:

> It's a matter of training, of many years of attentive listening, and then involuntarily you start to write "by sound"— paronomastically, anagrammatically, with luxuriant rhythms (all these naturally similar phenomena). Essentially, the semantic composition of the poem is a phenomenon isomorphic with these "sound" bits, and it is more the result of practical skill than of conscious design.[30]

In general, it has not been possible for me to recreate the assonance and internal rhymes; they have been sacrificed for the sake of semantic adequacy. Likewise, the metrical schemes have largely not been reproduced for the same reason. I've maintained general stanza structure and, whenever possible, rhythmic flow. Opting for semantic fidelity, the translations collected here are more or less literal renditions that retain as much as possible of the meter, though not the patterns of rhyme. They are blank verse renditions, called "*belye stikhi*" in Russian: "white verse," the color, I hope, of a well-negotiated surrender. The translations are intended to convey some sense of the original to students of poetry who lack Russian and to Anglophone students of Russian whose understanding of the language is not sufficient to read Loseff independently. Notes to individual poems can merely suggest the rich

---

[29] For an introduction to these and other formal features of Russian verse, see B. O. Unbegaun, *Russian Versification* (Oxford: Clarendon Press, 1956); and for a more elaborate discussion, see Barry Scherr, *Russian Poetry: Meter, Rhythm, and Rhyme* (Berkeley: University of California Press, 1986).

[30] Quoted in Boris Paramonov, "Vyzhivanie poeta," *Grani* 140 (1986): 149–160, here p. 151.

and playful allusiveness of the original poems, which invoke Pushkin and contemporary émigré writers with equally deft familiarity. Clearly, a fully annotated edition of Loseff's poetry is required, and it is my fervent hope that fellow scholars will undertake such a project, to which the notes included here constitute a modest initial contribution.[31]

A Note on this Edition

Back in the mid-1980s Lev Loseff invited me to translate his poems into English for eventual publication. The vagaries of my biography forced me to set the project aside again and again, and I only wish he were alive now to receive this book as a gesture of respect and gratitude for his tuition and friendship. He selected the poems chiefly from his first two collections of verse: *Чудесный десант* and *Тайный советник*, both published by Hermitage (Tenafly, N.J.) in 1985 and 1987, respectively.[32] These poems have been checked and when necessary corrected against Loseff's collected verse *Собранное* (Ekaterinburg: U-Faktoriia, 2000). The uncollected poem, also selected by Loseff, was originally published in the émigré journal *Грани* (41, no. 139 [1986]: 85). My thanks to Dimitry Loseff for generous permission to reproduce his father's poems here.

Acknowledgments

Several colleagues, former students, and admirers of Loseff and his poetry have helped me in the final stages of this book with generous criticisms, suggestions, and support. My warmest thanks go to Mark Lipovetsky, Nathan Long, Slava Paperno, Rebecca Pyatkevich, Michael Wachtel and especially Barry Scherr and Timothy Sergay for their time and wisdom. All infelicities that remain are of course mine alone. My thanks to Eric Scace, Jessica Schilling, Tim Riggs, and Eric Walczak for assistance with design and graphics.

---

31 An indication of the extent of the project is given by an essay that traces out the many allusions inhabiting the poem "Pushkin Historical Sites": Aleksandr Zholkovskii, "'Puskinskie Mesta' L'va Loseva i ikh okrestnosti," *Zvezda* 2 (2008): 215–228; a revised English version is to appear in M. Gronas and B. Scherr (eds.), *Лифшиц/Лосев/Loseff/левлосев* (Moscow: Novoe literaturnoe obozrenie, forthcoming).

32 Loseff's subsequent volumes of poetry are: *Новые сведения о Карле и Кларе: Третья книга стихотворений* (1996); *Послесловие: Книга стихов* (1998); *Sisyphus redux: Пятая книга стихотворений* (2000); *Как я сказал: Шестая книга стихотворений* (2005); *Говорящий попугай. Седьмая книга стихотворений* (2009), all published by Puskinskii Fond in Saint Petersburg.

Drawing of Lev Loseff by Mikhail Belominsky, ca. 1974.

Selected Early Poems
Lev Loseff

СОДЕРЖАНИЕ

Из книги *Чудесный десант*

ПАМЯТИ ВОДКИ	2
Последний романс	4
Рота Эрота	6
Разговор с нью–йоркским поэтом	8
Нелетная погода	10
М	12
Петроградская сторона	16
Памяти Москвы	20
Памяти Пскова	22
«Понимаю — ярмо, голодуха…»	24
Чудесный десант	26
Памяти Литвы	30
«Под утро удалось заснуть, и вновь…»	32
Жалобы кота	34
Отлет	36
ПРОДЛЕННЫЙ ДЕНЬ	38
«Я ясно вижу дачу и шиповник…»	40
«Продленный день для стриженых голов…»	42
«Евгений Шварц пугливым юморком…»	46
«Над озером, где можно утонуть…»	48
«…в "Костре" работал. В этом тусклом месте…»	52
«Мой самый лучший друг и полувраг…»	56
«Покуда Мельпомена и Евтерпа…»	58
Подписи к виденным в детстве картинкам	62

CONTENTS

From *The Wondrous Raid*

In Memory of Vodka 3
The Last Romance 5
The Regiment of Eros 7
Conversation with a New York Poet 9
Grounded by Foul Weather 11
M 13
The Petrograd Side 17
In Memory of Moscow 21
In Memory of Pskov 23
"I know, the Mongol yoke, the years of famine…" 25
The Wondrous Raid 27
In Memory of Lithuania 31
"Towards morning I managed to fall asleep…" 33
A Cat's Lament 35
Departure 37

The Extended Day 39
"I clearly see the dacha and the dog rose…" 41
"An extended day for close-cropped heads…" 43
"With his timorous wisp of humor…" 47
"Above the lake, where one can easily drown…" 49
"I used to work for *Campfire*. In that dreary place…" 53
"My very best friend and half-enemy…" 57
"While Melpomene and Euterpe…" 59
Captions to Pictures Seen in Childhood 63

ПРОТИВ МУЗЫКИ — 68

«Лучок нарезан колесом…» — 70

Путешествие — 72

Бахтин в Саранске — 84

Истолкование Целкова — 88

Стансы — 90

Федра — 92

Слегка заплетаясь — 94

Ткань — 96

Открытка из Новой Англии. 1 — 100

Стихи о романе — 104

ПБГ — 110

Пушкинские места — 114

«Грамматика есть бог ума…» — 116

Классическое — 118

Документальное — 120

Инструкция рисовальщику гербов — 122

«Мы наблюдаем при солнца восходе…» — 124

«Земную жизнь пройдя до середины…» — 126

УРОК ФОТОГРАФИИ — 132

Москвичи — 134

Амфибронхитная ночь — 140

Разговор — 146

Письмо на родину — 148

«Тем и прекрасны эти сны…» — 150

На Рождество — 152

«И, наконец, остановка "Кладбище"…» — 154

«Нам звуки ночные давно невдомек…» — 156

Трамвай — 158

Марш — 162

Урок фотографии. 1 — 166

«Все пряжи рассучились…» — 168

В отеле — 170

Открытка из Новой Англии. 2 — 172

Against Music — 69
- "An onion in bandy slices…" — 71
- The Journey — 73
- Bakhtin in Saransk — 85
- An Interpretation of Tselkov — 89
- Stanzas — 91
- Phaedra — 93
- Slightly Stumbling — 95
- Cloth — 97
- Postcard from New England. 1 — 101
- Verses on the Novel — 105
- PBG — 111
- Pushkin Historical Sites — 115
- "Grammar is indeed the god of the mind…" — 117
- Classical — 119
- Documentary — 121
- Instructions to a Heraldic Illustrator — 123
- "With the rising of the sun we observe…" — 125
- "Midway in the journey of my earthly life…" — 127

Photography Lesson — 133
- Muscovites — 135
- Amphibronchic Night — 141
- Conversation — 147
- Letter to the Old Country — 149
- "And yet these dreams are beautiful…" — 151
- At Christmas — 153
- "And finally, the bus stop 'Cemetery'…" — 155
- "We'd long ago grown deaf to nocturnal sounds…" — 157
- The Tram — 159
- March — 163
- Photography Lesson. 1 — 167
- "All the threads have come undone…" — 169
- In the Hotel — 171
- Postcard from New England. 2 — 173

Сон	174
Открытка из Новой Англии. 3	176
«Я сна не торопил, он сразу состоялся...»	178
Местоимения	180
Урок фотографии. 2	182
«Дом наполнен теплом...»	184
«Что день, то повышается накал...»	186
Один день Льва Владимировича	188
Норковый ручей	196
Моя книга	202

Из книги *Тайный советник*

«Лебедь пота шипа ран»	206
3 рубля	210
DE PROFUNDIS	214
«Поэт есть перегной, в нем мертвые слова...»	216
В гроссбух	218
Левлосев	220
Двенадцать коллегий. Элегия в трех частях	222
«Стерва ворона закаркала...»	228

Несобранное

Аллегория	232

Dream	175
Postcard from New England. 3	177
"I did not hasten sleep, it happened at once…"	179
Pronouns	181
Photography Lesson. 2	183
"The house is filled with warmth…"	185
"Every day the intensity of confusion…"	187
One Day in the Life of Lev Vladimirovich	189
Mink Brook	197
My Book	203

From *Privy Councilor*

"The Swan of the Sweat of the Thorn of Wounds"	207
3 Rubles	211
De Profundis	215
"A poet is compost, in him dead words…"	217
In the Ledger	219
Levlosev	221
Twelve Colleges. An Elegy in Three Parts	223
"The raven's corpse began to caw…"	229

Uncollected

Allegory	233

Notes to Translations 235

Из книги *Чудесный десант*

From *The Wondrous Raid*

ПАМЯТИ ВОДКИ

In Memory of Vodka

ПОСЛЕДНИЙ РОМАНС

Юзу Алешковскому

> Не слышно шуму городского,
> В заневских башнях тишина!
> *Ф. Глинка*

Над невской башней тишина.
Она опять позолотела.
Вот едет женщина одна.
Она опять подзалетела.

Все отражает лунный лик,
воспетый сонмищем поэтов,—
не только часового штык,
но много колющих предметов.

Блеснет Адмиралтейства шприц,
и местная анестезия
вмиг проморозит до границ
то место, где была Россия.

Окоченение к лицу
не только в чреве недоноску,
но и его недоотцу,
с утра упившемуся в доску.

Подходит недорождество,
мертво от недостатка елок.
В стране пустых небес и полок
уж не родится ничего.

Мелькает мертвый Летний сад.
Вот едет женщина назад.
Ее искусаны уста.
И башня невская пуста.

The Last Romance

for Yuz Aleshkovsky

> Unheard is the city's din,
> Quiet are the towers across the Neva.
> F. Glinka

All is still above the Neva tower.
Once again it's turned to gold.
There's a woman riding alone.
Once again she's knocked up.

All is reflected in the face of the moon
(praised in song by swarms of poets)—
not only the sentry's bayonet,
but many other sharp instruments.

The syringe of the Admiralty flashes,
and the local anesthetic
instantly extends to the borders
and numbs the place where Russia once was.

The numbness suits quite well
the premature baby in the womb,
but also its premature father,
plastered drunk since morning.

We're in for a stillborn Christmas,
cause of death: a lack of fir trees.
In the land of empty skies and shelves,
absolutely nothing will be born.

A glimpse of the dead Summer Gardens.
There's the woman coming back.
On her swollen lips are teeth marks.
And the Neva tower is empty.

РОТА ЭРОТА

Нас умолял полковник наш, бурбон,
пропахший коньяком и сапогами,
не разлеплять любви бутон
нетерпеливыми руками.
А ты не слышал разве, блядь, —
не разлеплять.

Солдаты уходили в самовол
и возвращались, гадостью налившись,
в шатер, где спал, как Соломон,
гранатометчик Лева Лифшиц.
В полста ноздрей сопели мы —
он пел псалмы.

«В ландшафте сна деревья завиты,
вытягивается водокачки шея,
две безымянных высоты,
в цветочках узкая траншея».
Полковник головой кивал:
бряцай, кимвал!

И он бряцал: «Уста — гранаты, мед —
ее слова. Но в них сокрыто жало…»
И то, что вставлял в гранатомет,
летело вдаль, но цель не поражало.

The Regiment of Eros

Our colonel, the lout,
reeking of cognac and boot leather,
begged us not to snap the bud of love
with impatient hands.
What the fuck, you didn't hear?—
don't snap it off.

The soldiers would go AWOL
and return, brimming with rotgut,
to the tent where Grenadier Lyova Lifshits
slept like King Solomon.
We wheezed through fifty nostrils—
he would sing psalms.

"In the landscape of dream the trees are twisted,
the neck of the water tower stretches upward,
two nameless heights,
and a slit trench covered in flowers."
The colonel nodded:
Tinkle on, cymbal!

And he tinkled: "Her lips are grenadillas,
and honey are her words. But a sting hides within . . ."
And what he inserted into the grenade launcher
flew far, but failed to damage the target.

РАЗГОВОР С НЬЮ-ЙОРКСКИМ ПОЭТОМ

Парень был с небольшим приветом.
Он спросил, улыбаясь при этом:
«Вы куда поедете летом?»

– Только вам. Как поэт поэту.
Я в родной свой город поеду.
Там источник родимой речи.
Он построен на месте встречи
Элефанта с собакой Моськой.
Туда дамы ездят на грязи.
Он прекрасно описан в рассказе
А. П. Чехова «Дама с авоськой».

Я возьму свой паспорт еврейский.
Сяду я в самолет корейский.
Осеню себя знаком креста —
и с размаху в родные места!

Conversation with a New York Poet

The fellow has a screw loose.
He asked, smiling all the while,
"Where are you going for the summer?"

—I'll tell just you. One poet to another.
I'm going to my hometown,
the source of my native speech.
My town's built on the site of a meeting
between an elephant and a pug dog.
Ladies sojourn there for the mud-baths.
The town is perfectly depicted in the tale
by Anton Chekhov, "Lady with a Handbag."

I'll bring my Jewish passport,
and board a Korean airliner,
bless myself with the sign of the cross—
and away to my native land!

НЕЛЕТНАЯ ПОГОДА

Где некий храм струился в небеса,
теперь там головешки, кучки кала
и узкая канала полоса,
где Вытегра когда-то вытекала
из озера. Тихонечко бася,
ползет буксир. Накрапывает дрема.
Последняя на область колбаса
повисла на шесте аэродрома.
Пилот уже с утра залил глаза
и дрыхнет, завернувшись в плащ-палатку.
Сегодня нам не улететь. Коза
общипывает взлетную площадку.
Спроси пилота, ну зачем он пьет,
он ничего ответить не сумеет.
Ну, дождик. Отменяется полет.
Ну, дождик сеет. Ну, коза не блеет.

Коза молчит и думает свое,
и взглядом пожелтелым от люцерны,
она низводит наземь воронье,
освобождая небеса от скверны,
и тут же превращает птичью рать
в немытых пэтэушников команду.
Их тянет на пожарище пожрать,
пожарить девок, потравить баланду.
Как много их шагает сквозь туман,
бутылки под шинелками припрятав,
как много среди юных россиян
страдающих поносом геростратов.

Кто в этом нас посмеет укорить —
что погорели, не дойдя до цели.

Пилот проснулся. Хочется курить.
Есть «беломор». Но спички отсырели.

Grounded by Foul Weather

Where once a temple streamed into the sky
now are only smoldering brands, clumps of dung,
and the narrow strip of a canal
where once the Vytegra used to flow
from the lake. Murmuring in a bass voice,
a tug boat crawls along. It's drizzling drowsiness.
The last sausage in the region
droops from the aerodrome's pole.
The pilot's been soused since morning,
and dozes, wrapped in his tent-poncho.
We can't fly today. The goat
tugs here and there at the runway.
Go and ask the pilot why he's drinking,
he won't even be able to answer.
Ah well, some rain. The flight's cancelled.
Ah, it's still drizzling. Well, the goat's not bleating.

The goat quietly keeps to its own thoughts,
and with a glance alfalfa-jaundiced,
brings the crows to the ground,
delivering the skies from filth,
and transforming the feathered host
into a gang of unwashed PTUers.
They long to get soused amid the charred remains,
screw the wenches and shoot the shit.
So many of them march through the mist
with bottles safely hidden under shabby overcoats,
Among the youth of Russia, so many
Herostratuses suffering from diarrhea.

Who would dare reproach us
for crapping out short of our goal?

The pilot's awake. He wants to smoke.
He's got some Belomors. But his matches are damp.

М

М-М-М-М-М-М — кирпичный скалозуб
над деснами под цвет мясного фарша
несвежего. Под звуки полумарша
над главным трупом ходит полутруп.

Ну, Капельдудкин, что же ты, валяй,
чтоб застучали под асфальтом кости —
котлетка Сталина, протухшая от злости,
Калинычи и прочий де-воляй.

М-М-М-М-М-М — кремлевская стена,
морока и московское мычанье.
Милиционер мне сделал замечание,
что, мол, негоже облегчаться на

траву вблизи бессмертной мостовой,
где Ленина видал любой булыжник.
Сказал, что оскорбляю чувства ближних.
Но не забрал гуманный постовой.

Конечно, праздник — пьянка и расход:
летят шары, надуты перегаром,
и вся Москва под красным пеньюаром
корячится. Но это же раз в год.

На девушек одних в такие дни
уходит масса кумача и ваты,
и у парней, рыжи и кудреваты,
прически вылезают из мотни.

Раз в год даешь разгул, доступный всем.
Ура, бумажный розан демонстраций.
Но вот уж демон власти, рад стараться,
усталым зажигает букву М.

M

M-M-M-M-M-M—a brick-red snigger
above gums the color of overripe
ground meat. The half-dead march
to a half-march above the cadaver-in-chief.

Well, pied piper, what are you up to, get going,
so that the bones begin to knock under the asphalt;
Stalin cutlet, gone bad from malice, and
the Kalinin clan and other de volaille.

M-M-M-M-M-M—the Kremlin wall,
the muddle and the Moscow mooing.
A militia man reprimanded me,
saying it's improper to relieve myself

on the grass beside the eternal pavement,
where every cobblestone had witnessed Lenin.
He said I'm offending the next of kin.
But the kindly officer didn't take me in.

A holiday means drink and costly cheer:
balloons fly, full of liquored breath, and all
of Moscow squats under a red peignoir.
After all, it's only once a year.

On days like this the girls alone
consume tons of red calico and cotton,
while the coiffures of the boys,
curly and russet, peek out of open flies.

Let's have a bash once a year, open to everyone.
Hooray, a paper rose of parades.
But already the demon of power, at your service sir,
lights up on the "M" for all the tired ones.

Вот город. Вот портреты в пиджаках.
Вот улица. Вот нищие жилища.
Желудком не удержанная пища.
Лучинки в леденцовых петушках.

Вот женщина стоит — подобье тумбы
афишной и снаружи и внутри,
и до утра к ней прислонились три
пигмея из мучилища Лумумбы.

М

There's the city. There're the portraits in dress jackets.
There's the street. There are the tenements.
Food the stomach couldn't keep down.
Tiny splinters in the lollipop roosters.

Over there a woman is standing, the likeness
of an advertising column both inside and out,
and three pygmies from Lumumba Puniversity
slumped against her until morning.

И

ПЕТРОГРАДСКАЯ СТОРОНА

> Доходят ли до тебя мои письма?
> Я по-прежнему ...
> *М.*

По воскресеньям дети шли проверить,
по-прежнему ли плавают в бассейне
размокший хлеб с конфетною оберткой,
по-прежнему ли к проволоке вольера
приклеены пометом пух и перья,
по-прежнему ли подгнивает кость
на отсыревших от мочи опилках,
по-прежнему ли с нечеловеческой тоской
ревет кассирша в деревянной клетке.

Все оставалось на своих местах.
Палила пушка, но часы стояли.
Трамвай бренчал, но не съезжал с моста.
Река поплескивала, но не текла.
И мы прощались, но не расставались.
И только пресловутый невский ветер
куражился на диком перекрестке
меж зданий государственной мечети,
конструктивистского острога и
храмоподобья хамовитой знати,
насилуя прохожих в подворотнях,
так беспощадно плащи срывая, *что
казался одушевленным.*

The Petrograd Side

> Do my letters reach you?
> I'm still the same . . .
> M.

On Sundays the children would go to check
whether sodden bread in a candy wrapper
still floats in the pool,
and whether down and feathers
still cling to the dung on the voliere's wire,
and whether the bone is still rotting
on the sawdust damp with urine,
and whether the cashier girl still howls
with inhuman despair in her wooden cage.

Everything remained in its place.
The canon fired, but the clock had stopped.
The tram hummed, but did not leave the bridge.
The river plashed, but did not flow.
And we bid each other farewell, but did not part.
And only the notorious Neva wind
was swaggering at a wild intersection
midst the buildings of a state mosque,
a constructivist jail and
a temple-like thing of the boorish nobility,
assaulting passersby in the archways,
ripping away raincoats so mercilessly,
that it seemed to be alive.

Но ветер вдруг в парадной помер.
Подошел трамвай мой номер.
Все задвигалось, пошло.
И это все произошло
с поспешностью дурацкого экспромта.

Друг в прошлое запрыгал на ходу,
одной ногой в гноящемся аду,
другой ногой на движущемся чем-то.

But the wind suddenly died against the front door.
My tram arrived.
Everything began to move and get going again.
And all of this took place
with the haste of a foolish impromptu remark.

A friend leaped into the past without stopping,
one foot in festering hell,
the other on something moving.

ПАМЯТИ МОСКВЫ

Длиннорукая самка, судейский примат.
По бокам заседают диамат и истмат.
Суд закрыт и заплечен.

В гальванической ванне кремлевский кадавр
потребляет на завтрак дефицитный кавьяр,
растворимую печень.

В исторический данный текущий момент
весь на пломбы охране истрачен цемент,
прикупить нету денег.

Потому и застыл этот башенный кран.
Недостройка. Плакат
«Пролетарий всех стран, не вставай с четверенек!»

In Memory of Moscow

A long-armed female of the species, the judge's primate.
On her flanks preside *Diamat* and *Histmat*.
The court is closed and with "executive" powers.

In a galvanic bath the Kremlin cadaver
consumes for breakfast rare *caviar*
and instant liver.

At this historical present moment in time
all the cement went to tooth fillings for the guards,
and there's no money to buy more.

And that's why this crane has come to a standstill.
Construction halted. A poster:
"Workers of the World, Don't Arise from Your Hands and Knees!"

ПАМЯТИ ПСКОВА

Когда они ввели налог на воздух
и начались в стране процессы йогов,
умеющих задерживать дыхание
с намерением расстроить госбюджет,
я, в должности инспектора налогов
натрясшийся на газиках совхозных
(в ведомостях блокноты со стихами),
торчал в райцентре, где меня уж нет.

Была суббота. Город был в крестьянах.
Прошелся дождик и куда-то вышел.
Давали пиво в первом гастрономе,
и я сказал адье ведомостям.
Я отстоял свое и тоже выпил,
не то чтобы особо экономя,
но вообще немного было пьяных:
росли грибы с глазами там и сям.

Вооружившись бубликом и Фетом,
я сел на скате у Гремячей башни.
Река между Успеньем и Зачатьем
несла свои дрожащие огни.
Иной ко мне подсаживался бражник,
но, зная отвращение к поэтам
в моем народе, что я мог сказать им?
И я им говорил: «А ну дыхни».

In Memory of Pskov

When they levied a tax on the air
and trials began in the country against yogis
who are capable of holding their breath
with the intent of undermining the State budget,
I, in my capacity as tax inspector,
used to being bounced about in Kolkhoz Gaziks
(with notebooks of verse tucked into my official registers),
was hanging around the district center, where the grass is always greener.

It was Saturday. The town was full of peasants.
A rain shower came through and headed elsewhere.
They had beer in the first food shop,
and I bid the tax registers adieu.
I did my time in the line and also had a drink,
not that I was being particularly thrifty,
but there were only a few drunk people about:
here and there mushrooms with eyes were growing.

Armed with a bagel and Fet,
I sat on the slope near Gunpowder Tower.
The river between Assumption and Conception churches
bore along its tremulous lights.
A reveler or two would sit down next to me,
but, knowing the antipathy accorded poets by my people,
what could I say to them?
So I told them, "Alright, let's check your breath."

* * *

«Понимаю — ярмо, голодуха,
тыщу лет демократии нет,
но худого российского духа
не терплю», — говорил мне поэт.
«Эти дождички, эти березы,
эти охи по части могил», —
и поэт с выраженьем угрозы
свои тонкие губы кривил.
И еще он сказал, распаляясь:
«Не люблю этих пьяных ночей,
покаянную искренность пьяниц,
достоевский надрыв стукачей,
эту водочку, эти грибочки,
этих девочек, эти грешки
и под утро заместо примочки
водянистые Блока стишки;
наших бардов картонные копья
и актерскую их хрипоту,
наших ямбов пустых плоскостопье
и хореев худых хромоту;
оскорбительны наши святыни,
все рассчитаны на дурака,
и живительной чистой латыни
мимо нас протекала река.
Вот уж правда — страна негодяев:
и клозета приличного нет», —
сумасшедший, почти как Чаадаев,
так внезапно закончил поэт.
Но гибчайшею русскою речью
что-то главное он огибал
и глядел словно прямо в заречье,
где архангел с трубой погибал.

* * *

"I know, the Mongol yoke, the years of famine,
that we've gone a thousand years without democracy,
but I cannot stand the wretched
Russian spirit," a poet was telling me.
"The rain showers, the birches,
the sighs apropos of graves,"
and the poet curled his thin lips
into a threatening gesture.
Getting fired up, he continued:
"I hate these drunken evenings,
the penitential sincerity of drunks,
the Dostoevskian psychodrama of informers,
the vodka shots and mushroom tops,
the pretty girls, the petty sins,
and, come morning, instead of a cold compress,
the sodden rhymes of Blok;
the cardboard lances of our bards
and their well-rehearsed rasp,
the flat-footedness of our empty iambs
and the lameness of our haggard trochees.
Our rites and sanctities are insulting,
all designed for idiots,
and the life-bearing waters of Latin
flowed right past us.
There you have it: a land of scoundrels:
and there isn't even a proper WC."—
with that, raving almost like Chaadaev,
the poet suddenly broke off.
But with his most pliant Russian speech
he'd skirted something essential,
and gazed as if across a river,
where an archangel with a trumpet was dying.

ЧУДЕСНЫЙ ДЕСАНТ

Все шло, как обычно идет.
Томимый тоской о субботе,
толокся в трамвае народ,
томимый тоской о компоте,

тащился с прогулки детсад.
Вдруг ангелов Божьих бригада,
небесный чудесный десант
свалился на ад Ленинграда.

Базука тряхнула кусты
вокруг Эрмитажа. Осанна!
Уже захватили мосты,
вокзалы, кафе «Квисисана».

Запоры тюрьмы смещены
гранатой и словом Господним.
Заложники чуть смущены —
кто спал,
        кто нетрезв,
                кто в исподнем.

Сюда — Михаил, Леонид,
три женщины, Юрий, Володи!
На запад машина летит.
Мы выиграли, вы на свободе.

Шуршание раненых крыл,
влачащихся по тротуарам.
Отлет вертолета прикрыл
отряд минометным ударом.

The Wondrous Raid

Everything was going along as it usually does.
Weary with longing for Saturday,
people elbowed each other in the tram.
Weary with longing for fruit cocktail,

the kindergarten slogged back from recess.
Suddenly a brigade of Holy angels,
a celestial, wondrous landing party,
descended upon the hell of Leningrad.

A bazooka blast shook the shrubs
around the Hermitage. Hosannah!
They've already taken the bridges,
the train stations, the café "Quisisana."

The gates of the prison were opened
with a grenade and the word of the Lord.
The hostages were slightly abashed:
Some were sleeping,
     some weren't completely sober,
          others were in their underwear.

Quick, this way: Mikhail, Leonid,
three women, Yuri, Volodyas!
We're flying to the West.
We've won, you're free.

A rustle of wounded wings,
dragged along the sidewalk.
A detachment covered the helicopter's
lift-off with a mortar round.

Но таяли силы, как воск,
измотанной ангельской роты
под натиском внутренних войск,
понуро бредущих с работы.

И мы вознеслись и ушли,
растаяли в гаснущем небе.
Внизу фонарей патрули
в Ульянке, Гражданке, Энтеббе.

И тлеет полночи потом
прощальной полоской заката
подорванный нами понтон
на отмели подле Кронштадта.

But like wax, the strength
Of the exhausted angelic army
melted under the onslaught of the Interior troops,
shuffling home dejectedly from work.

And we ascended and left,
and melted into the ebbing light.
Below, the patrols of lanterns
in Ulyanka, Grazhdanka, Entebbe.

And far into the night, like
a parting ribbon of sunset,
smoldered the pontoon bridge we had blown up
on the sandbar along Kronstadt.

ПАМЯТИ ЛИТВЫ
Вальс

Дом из тумана, как дом из самана,
домик писателя Томаса Манна,
добрый, должно быть, был бурш.
Долго ль приладить колеса к турусам —
в гости за речку к повымершим пруссам
правит повымерший курш.

Лиф поправляет лениво рыбачка.
Shit-с на песке оставляет собачка.
Мне наплевать, хоть бы хны.
Видно, в горячую кровь Авраама
влита холодная лимфа саама,
студень угрюмой чухны.

И, на лице забывая ухмылку,
ясно так вижу Казиса и Милду
в сонме Данут и Бирут.
Знаете, то, что нам кажется раем,
мы, выясняется, не выбираем,
нас на цугундер берут.

Вымерли гунны, латиняне, тюрки.
В Риме руины. В Нью-Йорке окурки.
Бродский себе на уме.
Как не повымереть. Кто не повымер.
«Умер» зудит, обезумев, как «immer»,
в долгой зевоте jamais.

In Memory of Lithuania
(a waltz)

A house of mist, like a house of adobe,
the chalet of Thomas Mann,
most likely, he was a good *Bursche*.
Will it take long to hitch up this load of nonsense?
An extinct Kursh heads across the river
to visit the extinct Prussians.

The fisherman's wife lazily adjusts her bodice.
On the beach the dog leaves shits.
Damn it all for all I care.
Apparently into the hot blood of Abraham
is mixed the cold lymph of the Lapp,
the galantine of morose Finns.

And forgetting the smirk on my face,
I clearly see Kazis and Milda
among the crowd of Danutas and Birutas.
You know, what seems like paradise to us
is never something we choose ourselves,
but rather to which we're hauled away.

They all died out: the Huns, the Latins, the Turks.
There are ruins in Rome. Cigarette butts in New York.
Brodsky's a crafty devil.
Of course you're going to die out. Who hasn't?
"He's dead" itches, out of its mind, like "*immer*,"
and in a long yawn—"*jamais*."

* * *

      А лес в неведомых дорожках —
      на деле гроб.
      Так нас учил на курьих ножках
      профессор Пропп.

Под утро удалось заснуть, и вновь
я посетил тот уголок кошмара,
где ко всему привычная избушка
переминается на курьих ножках,
привычно оборачиваясь задом
к еловому щетинистому лесу
(и лес хрипит, и хлюпает, и стонет,
медвежеватый, весь в сержантских лычках,
отличник пограничной службы — лес),
стоит, стоит, окошками моргает
и говорит: *«Сия дуэль ужасна!»*
К чему сей сон? При чем здесь Алешковский?
Куда идут ремесленники строем?
Какому их обучат ремеслу?
Они идут навстречу.
      Здравствуй, племя
младое, незнакомое. Не дай
мне Бог увидеть твой могучий
возраст …

* * *

>But a forest full of mysterious paths
>is in fact a coffin.
>Thus were we taught by chicken-legged
>Professor Propp.

Towards morning I managed to fall asleep,
and once again I visited that corner of the nightmare
where a cottage accustomed to everything
shifts from one chicken foot to the other,
habitually turning its backside
to the bristling forest of firs
(and the forest wheezes, and snorts, and groans,
a bit like a bear, complete with sergeant's stripes,
that paragon of border duty, the forest),
and stands and waits, winking with its tiny windows,
and says: "This duel is horrible!"
What's the point of this dream? What's Aleshkovsky got to do with it?
Where are these trade schoolers marching to?
What trade are they being taught?
They are coming towards me.
            Greetings,
young, unknown tribe. God preserve me
from ever witnessing your coming of age.

ЖАЛОБЫ КОТА

Горе мне, муки мне, ахти мне.
Не утешусь ни кошкой, ни мышкой.
Ах, темно в октябре, ах, темней
в октябре, чем у негра под мышкой.

Черт мне когти оставил в залог.
Календарный листок отрываю.
Увяжи меня, жизнь, в узелок,
увези на коленях в трамвае.

Или, чтобы скорее, в такси.
И, взглянув на народа скопленье,
у сердитой старухи спроси:
«Кто последний на усыпленье?»

A Cat's Lament

Woe is me, O wretched, hapless me.
Neither in feline nor in mouse will I find succor.
Ah, how dark it is in October, alas, it's darker
in October than in a black man's armpit.

The devil pawned his claws with me.
I tear another day from the calendar.
Wrap me up, O Life, in a neat bundle,
and bear me away on your lap in a tram.

Or, faster yet, in a taxi.
And after surveying the assortment of people,
ask of the grumpy old lady,
"Who's last in line for being put to sleep?"

ОТЛЕТ

и как будто легко я по трапу бежал,
в то же самое время я как будто лежал
неподвижен и счастлив всерьез,
удивляясь, что лица склоненных опухли от слез;

и тогда вдруг что-то мелькнуло
                      в помертвелой моей голове,
я пальцами сделал латинское V
(а по-русски, состроил рога).
Помолитесь за меня, дурака.

Departure

and I seemed to be running easily up the ramp,
at the same time it was as if I were lying
motionless and earnestly happy,
amazed that the faces bent over me were swollen from crying;

and then suddenly something flashed in my morbid mind,
with my fingers I made a Latin V
(and, in Russian, the shape of horns).
Pray for me, a fool.

ПРОДЛЕННЫЙ ДЕНЬ

И ДРУГИЕ ВОСПОМИНАНИЯ О ХОЛОДНОЙ ПОГОДЕ

> На острове, хранящем имена
> увечных девочек из княжеского рода,
> в те незабвенные для сердца времена
> всегда стояла теплая погода.
>
> *Нина Мохова*

The Extended Day

and Other Recollections of Cold Weather

> On the island which preserves the names
> of crippled girls of princely ancestry,
> in those times which the heart never forgets
> it always was warm weather.
>
> *Nina Mokhova*

I

Я ясно вижу дачу и шиповник,
забор, калитку, ржавчину замка,
сатиновые складки шаровар,
за дерево хватаюсь, суевер.
Я ясно вижу — злится самовар,
как царь или какой-то офицер,
еловых шишек скушавший полковник
в султане лиловатого дымка.
Так близко — только руку протяни,
но зрелище порой невыносимо:
еще одна позорная Цусима,
японский флаг вчерашней простыни.

А на крыльце красивый человек
пьет чай в гостях, не пробуя варенья,
и говорит слова: «Всечеловек …
Арийца возлюби … еврей еврея …
Отсюда шаг один лишь, но куда?
До царства Божия? до адской диктатуры?»

Теперь опять зима и холода.
Оленей гонят хмурые каюры
в учебнике (стр. 23).
«Суп на плите, картошку сам свари».

Суп греется. Картошечка варится.
И опера по радио опять.
Я ясно слышу, что поют — арийцы,
но арии слова не разобрать.

I

I clearly see the dacha and the dog rose,
the fence, the gate, the rust on the lock,
the satin pleats of country trousers,
and superstitious, I reach out for some wood.
I see clearly: the furious samovar,
like a czar or some officer,
a colonel well-fed on pine cones,
in a plume of violet smoke.
It's so close—just reach out your hand,
but at times the vision is unbearable:
yet another shameful Tsushima,
the Japanese flag of last night's bedsheet.

And on the porch the handsome man
drinks tea while he visits, without trying the jam,
and says the words: "Universal Man . . .
love an Aryan . . . and a Jew a Jew . . .
From here it's but one short step—but to what?
To the Kingdom of God? Or a hellish dictatorship?"

Now again it's winter and cold.
The sullen Lapps drive on
the reindeer teams in the schoolbook (p. 23).
"The soup's on the stove. Cook the potatoes yourself."

The soup is warming up. The potatoes are cooking.
And opera on the radio again.
And I clearly recognize the voices of Aryans,
though the words of the aria are indistinct.

II

Продленный день для стриженых голов
за частоколом двоек и колов,
там, за кордоном отнятых рогаток,
не так уж гадок.

Есть много средств, чтоб уберечь тепло,
помимо ваты в окнах и замазки.
Неясно, как сквозь темное стекло,
я вижу путешествие указки
вниз, по маршруту перелетных птиц,
под взглядами лентяев и тупиц.
На юг, на юг, на юг, на юг, на юг.
Оно надежней, чем двойные рамы.
Напрасно академия наук
нам посылает вслед радиограммы.
«Я полагаю, доктор Ливингстон?»
В ответ счастливый стон.

Края, где календарь без января,
где прикрывают срам листочком рваным,
где существуют, обезьян варя,
рассовывая фиги по карманам.
Мы обруселых немцев имена
подарим этим островам счастливым,
засим вернемся в город над заливом —
есть карта полушарий у меня.

II

An extended day for close-cropped heads,
beyond the palisades of D's and F's,
beyond the cordon of confiscated slingshots,
is not so lousy.

There are many means of conserving heat
besides cotton wadding in window seams and putty.
Indistinctly, as through a glass darkly,
I see the pointer travel downward,
along the route of migratory birds,
under the gazes of sluggards and dolts,
to the south, the south, the south.
It's more reliable than double-paned windows.
In vain the Academy of Sciences
forwards us radio messages.
"Doctor Livingstone, I presume?"
A happy groan in reply.

The regions where the calendar's missing January,
where they cover their shame with a shred of leaf,
where they live on boiled chimpanzee
and figs stuffed into pockets.
We will bestow upon these happy isles
the names of Russified Germans,
thereafter we'll return to the city on the gulf—
I have a map of the hemispheres with me.

Вот желтый крейсер с мачтой золотой
посередине северной столицы.
В кают-компании трубочный застой.
Кругом висят портреты пустолицы.
То есть уже готовы для мальца
осанка, эполет под бакенбардом,
история побед над Бонапартом
в союзе с Нельсоном и дырка для лица.

Посвистывает боцман-троглодит.
На баке кок толкует с денщиками.
Со всех портретов на меня глядит
очкастый мальчик с толстыми щеками.

There's the yellow cruiser with the golden mast
in the center of the northern capital.
Stale pipe smoke stagnates in the wardroom.
On the walls hang portraits with empty faces.
That is, already prepared for the lad are:
the bearing, the epaulettes below the side-whiskers,
the history of victories against Bonaparte in alliance with Nelson,
and a hole in which to stick his face.

The boatswain-troglodyte is whistling idly.
On the forecastle the cook holds forth with the batmen.
And staring down at me from all the portraits
is the bespectacled boy with plump cheeks.

III

Евгений Шварц пугливым юморком
еще щекочет глотки и ладоши,
а кто-то с гардеробным номерком
уже несется получить галоши.
И вот стоит, закутан до бровей,
ждет тройку у Михайловского замка,
в кармане никнет скомканный трофей —
конфетный фантик, белая программка.

Опущен занавес. Погашен свет.
Смыт грим. Повешены кудель и пакля
на гвоздик до вечернего спектакля.
В театре хорошо, когда нас нет.
Герой, в итоге победивший зло,
бредет в буфет, талончик отрывая.
А нам сегодня крупно повезло:
мы очень скоро дождались трамвая.

Вот красный надвигается дракон,
горят во лбу два разноцветных глаза.
И долго-долго, до проспекта Газа,
нас будет пережевывать вагон.

III

With his timorous wisp of humor
Evgeny Shvarts is still tickling throats and palms,
but already someone with a cloakroom claim check
is rushing off to receive his galoshes.
And there he stands, muffled up to the eyebrows,
waiting for the Number 3 at Mikhailovsky Castle,
as the crumpled spoils—a bonbon wrapper
and a white program—settle in his pocket.

The curtain is lowered. The lights are extinguished.
The grease paint is removed. The tow and hemp are
hung up on the nail until the evening performance.
It's good in the theatre, when we aren't there.
The hero, having triumphed over evil in the end,
ambles toward the refreshment bar, tearing off a ration coupon.
While today we were really lucky:
we hardly had to wait for the tram.

Lo, the red dragon looms near,
two motley eyes burning in his brow.
And for a long time, all the way to Gaz Avenue,
the tram car will chew on us.

IV

> И он, трепеща от любви и от близкой
> Смерти ...
> *В. Жуковский*

Над озером, где можно утонуть,
вдоль по шоссе, где могут раскорежить,
под небом реактивных выкрутас
я увидал в телеге тряской лошадь
и понял, в травоядное вглядясь,
что это дело можно оттянуть.
Все было, как в краю моем родном,
где пахнет сеном и собаки лают,
где пьют за Русь и ловят карасей,
где Клавы с Николаями гуляют,
где у меня полным-полно друзей.
Особенно я вспомнил об одном.

Неслыханный мороз стоял в Москве.
Мой друг был трезв, задумчив и с получки.
Он разделял купюры на две кучки.
Потом, подумав, брал с собою две.
Мы шли с ним в самый лучший ресторан,
куда нас недоверчиво впускали,
отыскивали лучший столик в зале,
и всякий сброд мгновенно прирастал.
К исходу пира тяжелел народ,
и только друг мой становился легок.
Тут выяснялось, что он дивный логик
и на себя все объяснить берет.

IV

> And he, trembling from love
> And death at hand...
> V. Zhukovsky

Above the lake, where one can easily drown,
along the highway, where one can always crash,
under a sky of intricate jet vapor trails,
I saw a horse before a rickety cart,
and realized, peering at the herbivore,
that this matter could be put off.
It was just like my native parts,
where it smells of hay and the dogs bark,
where folks drink to Russia and fish for carp,
where girls named Klava date boys named Nikolai,
and where it's crammed full of my friends.
I thought of one in particular.

It was freezing in Moscow like never before.
My friend was sober, pensive, and had just been paid.
He divided the bills into two piles.
Then, having thought a bit, he took both with him.
We went to the very best restaurant,
were admitted distrustfully,
and chose the best table in the room,
and instantly all kinds of riffraff latched on to us.
Towards the conclusion of the feast everyone was sluggish,
only my friend was lighter.
It then became clear that he's a wondrous logician,
and he took it upon himself to explain everything.

Он поднимался в свой немалый рост
средь стука вилок, кухонной вонищи
и говорил: «Друзья, мы снова нищи
и это будет наш прощальный тост.
Так выпьем же за стройный ход планет,
за Пушкина, за русских и евреев
и сообщением порадуем лакеев
о том, что смерти не было и нет».

He rose to his not inconsiderable height,
amid the clatter of forks and the kitchen stench,
and said, "Friends, once again we're destitute,
and this will be our farewell toast.
So let's drink to the harmonious course of the planets,
to Pushkin, to the Russians, and the Jews,
and let us brighten the hearts of the staff here
with the news that there is no death and never was."

V

... в «Костре» работал. В этом тусклом месте,
вдали от гонки и передовиц,
я встретил сто, а, может быть, и двести
прозрачных юношей, невзрачнейших девиц.
Простуженно протискиваясь в дверь,
они, не без нахального кокетства,
мне говорили: «Вот вам пара текстов».
Я в их глазах редактор был и зверь.
Прикрытые немыслимым рваньем,
они о тексте, как учил их Лотман,
судили как о чем-то очень плотном,
как о бетоне с арматурой в нем.
Все это были рыбки на меху
бессмыслицы, помноженной на вялость,
но мне порою эту чепуху
и вправду напечатать удавалось.

Стоял мороз. В Таврическом саду
закат был желт, и снег под ним был розов.
О чем они болтали на ходу,
подслушивал недремлющий Морозов,
тот самый, Павлик, сотворивший зло.
С фанерного портрета пионера
от холода оттрескалась фанера,
но было им тепло.

V

I used to work for *Campfire*. In that dreary place,
far from the hustle and the lead stories,
I met a hundred, maybe two hundred
pale young men and extremely plain maidens.
Coughing and shoving their way through the doorway,
and not without a brazen coquetry they'd say,
"Here're a couple of texts for you."
In their eyes I was an editor and a brute.
Dressed in unthinkable tatters,
they conceived of texts, as Lotman had taught them,
as if they were something solid,
like a cement pillar with metal reinforcement.
All this was only squared circles
of nonsense, multiplied by apathy,
but from time to time I actually managed
to get some of this rubbish printed.

It was freezing cold. In the Tavrichesky Garden
the sunset was yellow, and the snow beneath was rose.
The ever vigilant Morozov, that same Pavlik
who wrought evil, was eavesdropping
on them chatting on their walk.
The cold had caused the veneer to flake off
of a veneered portrait of the young pioneer,
but they were warm.

И время шло.
И подходило первое число.
И секретарь выписывал червонец.
И время шло, ни с кем не церемонясь,
и всех оно по кочкам разнесло.
Те в лагерном бараке чифирят,
те в Бронксе с тараканами воюют,
те в психбольнице кычат и кукуют,
и с обшлага сгоняют чертенят.

                And time passed.
And the first of the month would come.
And the secretary would sign the ledger and hand out a tenner.
And time passed, showing no favorites,
and scattered everyone across the tussocks.
Those in the camp barracks get high on *chifir*,
those in the Bronx battle the cockroaches,
those in the mental wards caw and coo-coo,
and shake demons from their cuffs.

VI

Мой самый лучший друг и полувраг
не прибирает никогда постели.
Ого! за разговором просидели
мы целый день. В окошке полумрак,
разъезд с работы, мартовская муть,
присутствие реки за два квартала,
и я уже хочу, чтоб что-нибудь
нас от беседы нашей оторвало,
но продолжаю говорить про долг,
про крест, но он уже далече.
Он, руки накрест, взял себя за плечи
и съежился, как будто он продрог.
И этим совершенно женским жестом
он отвергает мой простой резон.
Как проницательно заметил Гершензон:
«ущербное одноприродно с совершенством».

VI

My very best friend and half-enemy
never makes his bed.
But oh! We sat and talked
the whole day. Twilight in the window,
evening rush hour, March murkiness,
the presence of a river two blocks away,
and I already hope that something
will distract us from our conversation,
yet I go on talking of duty,
of the cross, but he's already farther off.
He crosses his arms and hugs his shoulders,
and huddles, as if chilled to the marrow.
And with this absolutely feminine gesture
he repudiates my simple argument.
With what insight Gershenzon remarked:
"The flawed and the perfect are of the same nature."

VII

Покуда Мельпомена и Евтерпа
настраивали дудочки свои,
и дирижер выныривал, как нерпа,
из светлой оркестровой полыньи,
и дрейфовал на сцене, как на льдине,
пингвином принаряженный солист,
и бегала старушка-капельдинер
с листовками, как старый нигилист,
улавливая ухом труляля,
я в то же время погружался взглядом
в мерцающую груду хрусталя,
нависшую застывшим водопадом:
там умирал последний огонек,
и я его спасти уже не мог.

На сцене барин корчил мужика,
тряслась кулиса, лампочка мигала,
и музыка, как будто мы — зека,
командовала нами, помыкала,
на сцене дама руки изломала,
она в ушах производила звон,
она производила в душах шмон
и острые предметы изымала.

VII

While Melpomene and Euterpe
were tuning their pipes,
and the conductor, like a seal, surfaced
from the bright orchestral icehole,
and the soloist, done up like a penguin,
drifted across the stage as if on an ice floe,
and the aging usherette rushed about
with leaflets like an old nihilist,
catching a few bars of "tralala,"
my gaze at that time was immersed
in the glittering heap of crystal
hanging like a frozen waterfall:
there the last spark was dying,
and I couldn't save it.

On stage a gentleman gave himself peasant airs,
the sidewings trembled, the lights flickered,
and the music was commanding us,
issuing orders, as if we were zeks,
on stage a lady was wringing her hands,
she caused a ringing in people's ears,
she caused a frisking of people's souls,
and removed sharp instruments.

Послы, министры, генералитет
застыли в ложах. Смолкли разговоры.
Буфетчица читала «Алитет
уходит в горы». Снег. Уходит в горы.
Салфетка. Глетчер. Мраморный буфет.
Хрусталь — фужеры. Снежные заторы.
И льдинами украшенных конфет
с медведями пред ней лежали горы.
Как я любил холодные просторы
пустых фойе в начале января,
когда ревет сопрано: «Я твоя!»,
и солнце гладит бархатные шторы.

Там, за окном, в Михайловском саду
лишь снегири в суворовских мундирах,
два льва при них гуляют в командирах
с нашлепкой снега — здесь и на заду.
А дальше — заторошена Нева,
Карелия и Баренцева лужа,
откуда к нам приходит эта стужа,
что нашего основа естества.
Все, как задумал медный наш творец, —
у нас чем холоднее, тем интимней,
когда растаял Ледяной дворец,
мы навсегда другой воздвигли — Зимний.

И все же, откровенно говоря,
от оперного мерного прибоя
мне кажется порою с перепоя —
нужны России теплые моря!

Ambassadors, ministers, generals, top brass
froze in their boxes. Conversations died away.
The snack bar salesgirl was reading *Alitet
Goes to the Hills*. Snow. Goes to the hills.
A napkin. A glacier. The marble buffet bar.
The crystal of the wine glasses. A snowy impasse.
And like ice floes of chocolates adorned
with bears, before her lay the mountains.
How I loved the chilly expanses
of empty foyers on the first days of January,
when the soprano roars: "I'm yours!"
and the sun strokes the velvet window curtains.

Through the window, in the Mikhailovsky Garden,
one sees only bullfinches in Suvorovesque full-dress uniforms,
two marble lions stroll among them as commanding officers,
with dollops of snow—here and on the rump.
And further off: the ice-packed Neva,
Karelia and the Barents puddle,
the source of this icy frost,
which is the basis of our nature.
All is as our bronze creator envisioned—
with us, the colder it is, the more intimate.
When the Ice Palace melted,
we built another to stand forever: the Winter Palace.

And nevertheless, to be perfectly honest,
due to the measured operatic surf,
or at times from too much drink, I think:
Russia does need access to warm seas!

ПОДПИСИ К ВИДЕННЫМ В ДЕТСТВЕ КАРТИНКАМ

1

Молился, чтоб Всевышний даровал
до вечера добраться до привала,
но вот он взобрался на перевал,
а спуска вниз как бы и не бывало.

Художник хмурый награвировал
верхушки сосен в глубине провала,
вот валунов одетый снегом вал
там, где вчера лавина пировала.

Летел снег вниз, летели мысли вспять,
в сон сенбернар вошел вразвалку с неким
питьем, чтоб было слаще засыпать
и крепче спать засыпанному снегом.

2

Болотный мох и бочажки с водой
расхристанный валежник охраняет,
и христианства будущий святой
застыл в кустах и арбалет роняет.

Он даже приоткрыл слегка уста,
трет лоб рукой, глазам своим не веря,
увидев воссияние креста
между рогов доверчивого зверя.

А как гравер изображает свет?
Тем, что вокруг снованье и слоенье
штрихов, а самый свет и крест — лишь след
отсутствия его прикосновенья.

Captions to Pictures Seen in Childhood

1

He offered prayers to the One on High,
that he might find shelter before evening,
but when he clambered up along the pass,
it seemed as if there were no way down.

The somber artist had engraved
the crests of the pines in the depths of the ravine,
the swell of boulders cloaked in snow,
where yesterday the landslide had feasted.

The snow flew down, and thoughts flew back,
a St. Bernard lumbered into his drowsiness
with a certain drink, so to slip sweetly
into sound sleep, smothered by the snow.

2

The windfallen brush, clad in tatters,
guards the marsh's pools and moss,
and a future saint of Christianity
stopped short in the bushes and drops his arbalest.

He's even opened his mouth slightly,
rubs his brow, not believing his eyes,
having seen the shining revelation of the cross
between the antlers of the trustful animal.

And how does the engraver represent the light?
By what is around the warping and layering of the strokes,
while the light itself and cross are only
the trace of the absence of his touch.

3

Штрих — слишком накренился этот бриг.
Разодран парус. Скалы слишком близки.
Мрак. Шторм. Ветр. Дождь. И слишком близко брег,
где водоросли, валуны и брызги.

Штрих — мрак. Штрих — шторм. Штрих — дождь. Штрих — ветра вой.
Крут крен. Крут брег. Все скалы слишком круты.
Лишь крошечный кружочек световой —
иллюминатор кормовой каюты.

Там крошечный нам виден пассажир,
он словно ничего не замечает,
он пред собою книгу положил,
она лежит, и он ее читает.

4

Змей, кольцами свивавшийся в дыре,
и тело, переплетшееся с телом, —
гравер, не поспевавший за Доре,
должно быть, слишком твердыми их сделал.

Крути картинку, сам перевернись,
но в том-то и загадочность спирали,
что не поймешь — ее спирали вниз
иль вверх ее могуче распирали.

Куда, художник, ты подзалетел —
что верх да низ! когда пружинит звонко
клубок переплетенных этих тел,
виток небес и адская воронка.

3

A stroke—this sloop is heeling too steeply.
The sail is ripped to shreds. The cliffs are too close.
Murk. Storm. Wind. Rain. And too close the shore,
with its seaweed, its boulders, its spray.

A stroke is murk. A stroke is storm. A stroke is rain. A stroke the
                                          howl of wind.
The steep heel. The steep shore. All the cliffs are too steep.
Only one tiny minute dot of light:
the porthole of the stern cabin.

There we can see a tiny passenger,
as if he notices nothing,
he's laid a book before him,
it lies there, and he reads it.

4

A snake, coiling upon itself in a pit,
and a body intertwined with another body—
the engraver, not up to Doré,
it seems, made the coils too hard.

Tilt the picture, even turn yourself around,
but something remains strange about the coils,
you can't figure out whether the picture's
being pressed downward or borne mightily upwards.

How, dear artist, could you botch it up so badly,
going upwards and downwards at the same time so,
while this tangle of intertwined bodies, this
coil of the heavens and funnel of Hell, tenses with an audible ring.

5

Мороз на стеклах и в каналах лед,
автомобили кашляют простудно,
последнее тепло Европа шлет
в свой крайний город, за которым тундра.

Здесь конькобежцев в сумерках едва
спасает городское освещенье.
Все знают — накануне Рождества
опасные возможны посещенья.

Куст роз преображается в куст льда,
а под окном, по краешку гравюры,
оленей гонят хмурые каюры.

Когда-нибудь я возвращусь туда.

5

There's frost on the windows and ice in the canals,
and autos cough as if caught cold,
Europe sends its last warmth
to her frontier city, on the edge of the tundra.

There the city lights barely save
the skaters in the twilight.
Everyone knows, on Christmas Eve
dangerous visitations are possible.

A rosebush is transformed into an icebush,
while under the window, at the very edge of the engraving,
sullen Lapps drive their reindeer teams.

Someday I'll return there.

ПРОТИВ МУЗЫКИ

Against Music

> Характерная особенность натюрмортов
> петербургской школы состоит в том, что
> все они остались неоконченными.
> *Путеводитель*

Лучок нарезан колесом. Огурчик морщится соленый. Горбушка горбится. На всем грубоватый свет зеленый. Мало свету из окна, вот и лепишь ты, мудила, цвет бутылки, цвет сукна армейского мундира. Ну, не ехать же на юг. Это надо сколько денег. Ни художеств, ни наук мы не академик. Пусть Иванов и Щедрин пишут миртовые рощи. Мы сегодня нашустрим чего-нибудь попроще. Васька, где ты там жива! Сбегай в лавочку, Васена, натюрморт рубля на два в долг забрать до пенсиона. От Невы неверен свет. Свечка. Отсветы печурки. Это, почитай, что нет. Нет света в Петербурге. Не отпить ли чутку лишь нам из натюрморта... Что ты, Васька, там скулишь, чухонская морда. Зелень, темень. Никак ночь опять накатила. Остается неоконч   Еще одна картина   Графин, графленный угольком, граненой рюмочки коснулся   знать художник   под хмельком   заснул   не проснулся

Л. Лосев (1937– ?). *НАТЮРМОРТ.*
Бумага, пиш. маш. Неоконч.

> A characteristic peculiarity of the
> Petersburg school of still lifes is
> that they remained unfinished.
> *Guidebook*

> An onion in bandy slices. A salted cucumber winces.
> A bread rind bends in round. Everything appears in a rather
> coarse green light. There's not enough light from the window,
> that's where you're lying, asshole: the color of the bottle, the color
> of the army uniform's cloth. Well, we won't go south. It costs too
> much. We're not members of the Academy of Arts nor of Sciences.
> Let Ivanov and Shchedrin go and paint myrtle bushes. Today we'll
> think up something simpler. Vaska, where the hell are you? Run
> over to the shop, Vasenka, and hock the still life for a couple of
> roubles, to carry us through 'til the check comes. That light from
> the Neva is shimmering. The candle. The reflected light of the stove.
> That, almost, doesn't exist. There's no light in Petersburg. If only
> we could just sip a bit out of the still life . . . What are you doing
> there, Vaska, whimpering with your lousy Finn mug. Greenness.
> Darkness. Looks like night has rolled round once again. It will
> remain unfinish   There's still another picture   A carafe,
> charcoal ruled, beside a faceted wineglass   know
> the artist   a little tipsy   he fell asleep   didn't wake up

L. Losev (1937–?). STILL LIFE.
Paper, typewriter. Unfinished.

ПУТЕШЕСТВИЕ

1. В прирейнском парке
            В. Максимову

            Я вылеплен не из такого теста,
            чтоб понимать мелодию без текста.
                    В. Уфлянд

В парке оркестр занялся дележом.
Палочкой машет на них дирижер,
распределяет за нотою ноту:
эту кларнету, а эту фаготу,
эту валторне, а эту трубе,
то, что осталось, туба, тебе.

В парке под сводами грабов и буков,
копятся горы награбленных звуков:
черного вагнера, красного листа,
желтого с медленносонных дерев —
вы превращаетесь в социалиста,
от изобилия их одурев.

Звуки без смысла. Да это о них же
предупреждал еще, помнится, Ницше:
«Ах, господа, гармоническим шумом
вас обезволят Шуберт и Шуман,
сладкая песня без слов, господа,
вас за собой поведет, но куда?»

В парке под музыку в толпах гуляк
мерно и верно мерцает гулаг,
чешутся руки схватиться за тачку,
в сердце все громче лопаты долбеж.
Что ж ты, душа, за простую подачку
меди гудящей меня продаешь?

THE JOURNEY

1. In a Park by the Rhine
for V. Maksimov

> I am not fashioned of such whey and curds
> As to understand a melody without words.
>   *V. Ufliand*

In the park the orchestra was working on the arrangement.
The conductor waves his baton at them,
allotting one note after the other:
this one to the clarinet, and that one to the bassoon,
this one to the French horn, and that one to the trumpet,
and what is left over to you, tuba.

In the park, under the arches of hornbeams and beeches
accumulate mountains of amassed sounds:
the black of wagner, the red of liszt,
yellow from the meddlesome trees;
you're turning into a socialist,
stupefied by their abundance.

The sounds have no meaning. But
remember, Nietzsche already warned us about that:
"Ah, gentlemen, Schubert and Schumann anesthetize
you with this harmonious noise,
the sweet song without words, gentlemen,
carries you away, but where to?"

In the park filled with music, amid the crowds of flaneurs
flashes the gulag, true and tried,
hands itching to grab the wheelbarrow,
the shovel's slap echoes ever louder in your heart.
What's with you, soul, you'll sell me out
for a simple scrap of sonorous copper?

2. В амстердамской галерее

К. Верхейлу

На руках у дамы умер веер.
У кавалера умолкла лютня.
Тут и подкрался к ним Вермеер,
тихая сапа, старая плутня.
Свет — но как будто не из окошка.
Европа на карте перемешалась.
Семнадцатый век — но вот эта кошка
утром в отеле моем ошивалась.

Как удлинился мой мир, Вермеер,
я в Оостенде жраал уустриц,
видел прелестниц твоих, вернее,
чтения писем твоих искусниц.
Что там в письме, не memento ли mori?
Все там будем. Но серым светом
с карты Европы бормочет море:
будем не все там, будем не все там.

В зале твоем я застрял, Вермеер,
как бы баркас, проходящий шлюзы.
Мастер спокойный, упрятавший время
в имя свое, словно в складки блузы.
Утро. Обратный билет уже куплен.
Поезд не скоро, в 16.40.
Хлеб надломлен. Бокал пригублен.
Нож протиснут меж нежных створок.

2. In an Amsterdam Gallery

for K. Verheul

The fan died in the lady's hands.
The cavalier's lute fell silent.
That's when Vermeer crept up to them
on the sly, up to his old tricks.
Light, but it seems not to come from the window.
Europe rearranged itself on the map.
The seventeenth century—but this morning that
cat was hanging around my hotel.

How my world lengthened, Vermeer,
I was in the Oostende deevoouring ooysters,
and saw your charming ladies, or, more likely,
the master readers of your letters.
What is not *memento mori*, there in the letter?
We'll all be there. But in the grey light
out of the map of Europe the sea mutters:
not everyone will be there, not everyone.

In your hall, Vermeer, I got held up,
like a barge in the sluice gates.
The peaceful master has concealed time
in his name, as if in the folds of a blouse.
Morning. The return ticket is already purchased.
There's time before the train at 16.40.
The bread's been broken, the goblet sipped from.
The knife wedged into the tender mussel.

3. В Английском канале

Т. и Д. Чемберс

Опухшее солнце Ла-Манша,
как будто я лишку хватил,
уставилось, как атаманша,
гроза коммунальных квартир.

Ну что ты цепляешься к Леше —
я пролил, так я и подтер.
Вон — ванночки, боты, калоши
захламили твой коридор.

Да, правда, нас сильно качает:
то к бару прильни, то отпрянь.
Я слышу начальника чаек
приказы, капризы и брань.

И я узнаю в ледоколе,
бредущем в Клайпеду, домой,
родные черты дяди Коли
с отвислой российской кормой.

Уже начинает смеркаться,
начальник своих разогнал,
а он начинает сморкаться —
о, трубный тоскливый сигнал!

Качается нос его красный,
а сзади, довольный собой,
висит полинялый и грязный
платочек его носовой.

3. In the English Channel

> *for T. and D. Chambers*

The swollen sun of *La Manche*,
as if I'd had one too many,
was staring at me, like a lady hetman,
the terror of communal apartments.

Now, why are you picking on Lyosha,
I spilled it, so I'll wipe it up.
Out there, bassinets, overshoes, and galoshes
clutter up your corridor.

You're right, we sure are rocking:
first lean towards the bar, then push backwards.
I hear the orders, whims, and curses
of the seagulls' commander.

And in the icebreaker wandering
homeward to Klaipeda, I recognize
Uncle Kolya's familiar features,
with his baggy Russian stern.

Dusk is already falling.
The commander has dispersed his squadron,
and Kolya begins to blow his nose—
O, that melancholy trumpet call!

His red nose swings and from
behind, self-contented, hangs
his dirty and faded
little handkerchief.

4. У женевского часовщика

С. Маркишу

В Женеве важной, нет, в Женеве нежной,
в Швейцарии вальяжной и смешной,
в Швейцарии, со всей Европой смежной,
в Женеве вежливой, в Швейцарии с мошной,
набитой золотом, коровами, горами,
пластами сыра с каплями росы,
агентами разведок, шулерами,
я вдруг решил: «Куплю себе часы».

Толпа бурлила. Шла перевербовка
сотрудников КЦГРБУ.
Но все разведки я видал в гробу.
Мне бы узнать, какие здесь штамповка,
какие на рубиновых камнях,
водоупорные и в кожаных ремнях.

Вдруг слышу из-под щеточки усов
печальный голос местного еврея:
«Ах, сударь, все, что нужно от часов,
чтоб тикали и говорили время».

«Чтоб тикали и говорили время…
Послушайте, вы это о стихах?»
«Нет, о часах, наручных и карманных…»
«Нет, это о стихах и о романах,
о лирике и прочих пустяках».

4. At a Geneva Watchmaker's

for S. Markish

In important Geneva, no, in tender Geneva,
in Switzerland impressive and ridiculous,
in Switzerland with all Europe contiguous,
in polite Geneva, in Switzerland with its purse
packed with gold, cows, mountains,
with slabs of cheese that have dewdrops,
with reconnaissance agents and cardsharps,
I suddenly decided, "I'll buy myself a watch."

The crowd was seething. The operatives
of the KCGIBA had all switched sides.
But I couldn't care less about all those spies.
I'd like to know, which here are factory-made,
which have ruby bearings,
are waterproof and with leather bands.

Suddenly I hear, from beneath a moustache's bristles,
the plaintive voice of the local Jew:
"Ach, sir, all that one needs from watches
is that they tick and tell time."

"That they tick and tell time . . .
Hey, are you talking about verse?"
"No, about watches, wristwatches and pocket watches . . ."
"No, that's about verses and novels,
about lyric poetry and other trifles."

5. В нормандской дыре

В. Марамзину

Не в первый раз волны пускались в пляс,
видно, они нанялись бушевать поденно,
и по сей день вижу я смуглый пляж,
плешь в кудельках, седых кудельках Посейдона.

Сей старичок отроду не был трезв,
рот разевает, и видим мы род трезубца,
гонит волну на Довиль, на Дюнкерк, на Брест,
зыбкие руки, руки его трясутся.

Это я помню с детства, с войны: да в рот
этих союзничков, русскою кровью, мать их.
Вот он полегший на пляжах второй фронт,
о котором мечтали на госпитальных кроватях.

Под пулеметы их храбро привел прилив.
Хитрый туман прикрывал корабли десанта.
Об этом расскажет тот, кто остался жив.
Кто не остался, молчит — вот что досадно.

Их имена, Господи, Ты веси,
сколько песчинок, нам ли их счесть, с размаху
мокрой рукой шлепнет прибой на весы.
В белом кафе ударник рванет рубаху.

В белом кафе на пляже идет гудьба.
Мальчик громит марсиан в упоении грозном.
Вилкой по водке писано: ЖИЗНЬ И СУДЬБА —
пишет в углу подвыпивший мелкий Гроссман.

Третью неделю пьет отпускник, пьет,
видно, он вьет, завивает веревочкой горе.
Бьет барабан. Бьет барабан. Бьет.
Море и смерть. Море и смерть. Море.

5. In the Norman Hole

for V. Maramzin

Not for the first time did the waves break into a dance,
apparently, they're paid to storm by the day,
and to this day I see the swarthy beach,
the bald spot among the ringlets, Poseidon's graying ringlets.

That old timer hasn't been sober a day of his life,
his mouth gapes open, and we see a sort of trident,
he drives a wave onto Deauville, Dunkirk, onto Brest,
his unsteady hands, his hands have the shakes.

This I recall from childhood, from the war: they suck,
these allies of ours, using Russian blood, -uck their mothers.
There it is at last, longed for by men in hospital beds,
the second front, mowed down on the beaches.

The tide bravely led them toward the machine guns.
The cunning mist was covering the ship's landing.
So it is told by those who survived.
Those who didn't keep silent, and that's annoying.

You, Lord, weigh their names—how could we tally them?—
the grains of sand that the surf, with a hard swing
of its wet hand slaps onto the scale.
In a white café a drummer tugs at his shirt.

In a white café on the beach there's a hubbub.
A boy in frightful rapture routs the Martians.
On a bottle, etched with a fork: Life and Fate—
a minor Grossman, tipsy, scribbles in the corner.

Three weeks the vacationer's been drinking, drinking,
apparently he's tying, packing up his troubles.
The drum beats. The drum beats. Beats.
Sea and death. Sea and death. Sea.

6. С собой на память

В. Казаку

Что я вспомню из этих дней и трудов —
с колоколен Кельна воскресную тишь,
некоторое количество немецких городов,
высокое качество остроконечных крыш,
одиночество, одиночество, одиночество, один
день за другим одиноким днем,
наблюдение за почтальоном из-за гардин,
почтовый ящик с рекламкой в нем,
превращение Америки в слово «домой»,
воркотню Би-Би-Си с новостями дня,
отсутствие океана между мной
и местом, где нет меня.

март — август 1984

6. A Keepsake for Yourself

for W. Kasack

What I'll recollect from these works and days:
the Sunday stillness after the Cologne bells,
a certain number of German cities,
the good quality of peaked roofs,
loneliness, loneliness, loneliness, one
lone day after another lonely day,
looking for the postman from behind the curtains,
the mailbox with a brochure in it,
the transformation of America into the word "home,"
the murmuring of the BBC with the news of the day,
the absence of the ocean between me
and the place where I'm not.

March–August 1984

БАХТИН В САРАНСКЕ

Капуцинов трескучие четки.
Сарацинов тягучие танцы.
Грубый гогот гог и магог.

«М. Бахтин, — говорили саранцы,
с отвращением глядя в зачетки, —
не ахти какой педагог».

Хотя не был Бахтин суевером,
но он знал, что в костюмчике сером
не студентик зундит, дьяволок:

«На тебя в деканате телега,
а пока вот тебе alter ego —
с этим городом твой диалог».

Мировая столица трахомы.
Обжитые клопами хоромы.
Две-три фабрички. Химкомбинат.

Здесь пузатая мелочь и сволочь
выпускает кислоты и щелочь,
рахитичных разводит щенят.

Здесь от храма распятого Бога
только щебня осталось немного.
В заалтарье бурьян и пырей.

Старый ктитор в тоске и запое
возникает, как клитор, в пробое
никуда не ведущих дверей.

Bakhtin in Saransk

The flashy rosaries of the Capuchins.
The languid dances of the Saracens.
The hoarse holler of the high and mighty.

"M. Bakhtin," said the Saranskens,
peering into the exam scores with revulsion,
"is not a particularly good teacher."

Although Bakhtin was not superstitious,
he did know that this was no student,
hissing in the grey suit, but a petty devil:

"Someone snitched on you at the dean's,
meanwhile here's your *alter ego*—
your dialogue with this city."

The world capital of trachoma.
Mansions habitable only by bedbugs.
Two or three factories. A chemical plant.

Here potbellied small fry and scum
manufacture acids and alkalis
and breed rachitic whelps.

Here only some detritus remains
from the temple of the crucified God,
tall weeds and couch grass in the sacristy.

Bored and drunk, the old church
warden rises, like a clitoris,
in the doorway that leads nowhere.

Вдоволь здесь погноили картошки,
книг порвали, икон попалили,
походили сюда за нуждой.

Тем вернее из гнили и пыли,
угольков и протлевшей ветошки
образуется здесь перегной.

Свято место не может быть пусто.
Распадаясь, уста златоуста
обращаются в чистый компост.

И протлевшие мертвые зерна
возрождаются там чудотворно,
и росток отправляется в рост.

Непонятный восторг переполнил
Бахтина, и профессор припомнил,
как в дурашливом давешнем сне

Голосовкер стоял с коромыслом.
И внезапно повеяло смыслом
в суете, мельтешенье, возне.

Все сошлось — этот город мордовский.
Глупый пенис, торчащий морковкой.
И звезда. И Вселенная вся.

И от глаз разбегались морщины.
И у двери толкались мордвины,
пересдачи зачета прося.

All over they'd left potatoes to rot,
torn up books, scorched icons,
and would come here at nature's call.

Thus more surely, from the filth and dust,
clumps of coal and moldy clothes,
humus grows here.

A sacred place cannot be empty.
Disintegrating, the lips of the golden-lipped
revert to pure compost.

And the dead and decaying grain
is miraculously reborn there,
and a sprout shoots forth.

An incomprehensible ecstasy overcame
Bakhtin, and the professor remembered
how in a silly dream of late,

Golosovker stood with a yoke and buckets.
And suddenly an idea stirred
amid the bustle, flickerings, and fussings.

Everything came together: this Mordvinian city.
The silly penis, sticking out like a carrot.
The star. And the whole universe.

And wrinkles darted out from his eyes.
And Mordvins were jostling each other at the door,
asking to retake the exam.

ИСТОЛКОВАНИЕ ЦЕЛКОВА

Ворс веревки и воск свечи.
Над лицом воздвижение зада.
Остальное — поди различи
среди пламени, мрака и чада.

Лишь зловеще еще отличим
в черной памяти-пламени красок
у Целкова период личин,
«лярв» латинских, по-нашему «масок».

Замещая ландшафт и цветы,
эти маски в прорехах и дырах
как щиты суеты и тщеты
повисали в советских квартирах.

Там безглазо глядели они,
словно некие антииконы,
как летели постылые дни,
пился спирт, попирались законы.

Но у кисти и карандаша
есть движение к циклу от цикла.
В виде бабочки желтой душа
на холстах у Целкова возникла.

Из личинок таких, что — хана,
из таких, что не дай Бог приснится,
посмотри, пролезает она
сквозь безглазого глаза глазницу.

Здесь присела она на гвозде,
здесь трассирует молниевидно.
На свече, на веревке, везде.
Даже там, где ее и не видно.

An Interpretation of Tselkov

The nap of some string and some candle wax.
The rearing up of a rump above a face.
As for the rest, just try to make it out
amid the flame, gloom, and oily smoke.

Only forebodingly can we make out
in the black memory-flame of paints
Tselkov's period of guises,
"larvae" in Latin, "masks" to us.

Replacing landscape and flowers,
these masks, torn and pocked,
hung in Soviet apartments
like shields of vacuity and vanity.

There, as if some kind of anti-icons,
they eyelessly observed
the passing of repellent days,
the flowing of alcohol and the flouting of laws.

But the brush and the pencil
have a movement from cycle to cycle.
A soul appeared in the form
of a yellow butterfly on Tselkov's canvasses.

Out of such larvae, which, God forbid
won't ever return to haunt our sleep,
look, the soul crawls through
the socket of an eyeless eye.

Here it sat awhile on the nail,
there it leaves its trace like lightning.
On the candle, on the string, everywhere.
Even there, where it's invisible.

СТАНСЫ

Расположение планет
и мрачный вид кофейной гущи
нам говорят, что Бога нет
и ангелы не всемогущи.

И все другие письмена,
приметы, признаки и знаки
не проясняют ни хрена,
а только топят все во мраке.

Все мысли в голове моей
подпрыгивают и бессвязны,
и все стихи моих друзей
безо́бразны и безобра́зны.

Когда по городу сную,
по делу или так гуляю,
повсюду только гласный У
привычным ухом уловляю.

Натруженный, как грузовик,
скулящий, как больная сука,
лишен грамматики язык,
где звук не отличим от звука.

Дурак, орущий за версту,
болтун, уведший вас в сторонку,
все произносят пустоту,
слова сливаются в воронку,

забулькало, совсем ушло,
уже слилось к сплошному вою.
Но шелестит еще крыло,
летящее над головою.

Stanzas

The arrangement of the planets
and the dismal look of the coffee grounds
tell us there is no God and
the angels are not omnipotent.

And all other characters,
portents, signs, and marks
don't clarify crap,
only drown everything in obscurity.

All the thoughts in my mind
bob around and are disjointed,
and all my friends' verses
are uncut and uncouth.

When I scurry about the city,
on business or out strolling,
I catch with my accustomed ear
from every side only the sound U.

Overworked like a truck,
whimpering like an ailing bitch,
the language's been stripped of grammar,
you can't tell one sound from the next.

The fool yelling from a mile away,
and the windbag drawing you aside,
they're all speaking emptiness,
the words flow into a funnel,

which gurgled, then was gone entirely,
already merged into a simple howl.
But a wing is still rustling,
fluttering overhead.

ФЕДРА

В каком-то музейном зале, помню —
занавеску отдернуть и снова завесить —
«Федра, охваченная любовью».

Федра, охваченная любовью;
вокруг народу человек десять:
пара кормилиц, пара поэтов,
полдюжины шарлатанов различной масти,
специалистов по даванию советов
по преодолению преступной страсти.

Ах, художник, скажи на милость,
зачем их столько сюда набилось?
В твоей гравюрке, художник, тесно,
здесь пахнет потом, а не искусством.

А просто всем поглядеть интересно
на Федру, охваченную столь странным чувством.

Phaedra

In a certain museum hall, I remember
(you pull aside a curtain, and afterwards draw it back)
"Phaedra Seized By Love."

Phaedra, seized by love;
around her a crowd of ten or more:
a couple of wet nurses, a couple of poets,
half a dozen charlatans of various stripes,
specialists in giving advice
on the surmounting of illicit passion.

Ah artist, if you please:
why are so many packed in there?
In your etching, sir, it's pretty cramped.
It smells of sweat, not of art.

But everyone is simply interested in having
a look at Phaedra, seized by such a bizarre feeling.

СЛЕГКА ЗАПЛЕТАЯСЬ

Льется дождь как из ведра.
Бог, рожденный из бедра,
победил меня сегодня
прямо с самого утра.

Не послать ли нам гонца?
Не заклать ли нам тельца?
То есть часть тельца (заклаем?) —
нам всего не съесть тельца.

Раздается странный стук.
Это я кладу в сундук —
то есть я кладу в кастрюлю
кость телячью, плоть и тук.[1]

Мой телец кипит, кипит.
Хочется с копыт, с копыт.
Но у нас еще графинчик
абсолютно не допит.

Эй, подать его сюды!
В нем награда за труды:
на две пятых — бог забвенья,
на три пятых — бог воды.[2]

---

1. Вырываю два листочка из лаврового венца.
2. Смысл стихотворения: в дождливый день автор пьет водку и варит телятину.
P.S. "Бог, рожденный из бедра" — Бахус.
P. P. S. Последние две строки — перифрастическое описание сорокаградусной водки.

Slightly Stumbling

It's raining buckets.
The god born of the thigh
vanquished me today,
right from early morning.

Should we send a messenger?
Should we sacrifice a calf?
that is, part of the calf (we'll sacrifice?):
we don't eat the whole calf.

A strange knocking is heard.
I'll put this in the cupboard—
that is, I'll put the calf bone,
meat and fat in the pot.[1]

My calf gets hotter and hotter.
While I totter and totter.
But we still have a carafe
that's yet to be quaffed.

Hey, serve it here!
Within is the reward for my labors:
two-fifths for the god of forgetfulness,
three-fifths for the god of water.[2]

---

1. I tear off two leaves from my laurel wreath.
2. The meaning of the poem: on a rainy day the author drinks vodka and cooks a veal cutlet.
P.S.: "The god born of the thigh" is Bacchus.
P.P.S.: The last two lines are a periphrastic description of 40-proof vodka.

ТКАНЬ
Докторская диссертация

1. *Текст* значит *ткань*[1]. Расплести по нитке тряпицу текста.
   Разложить по цветам, улавливая оттенки.
   Затем объяснить, какой окрашена краской
   каждая нитка. Затем — обсуждение ткачества ткани:
   устройство веретена, ловкость старухиных пальцев.   5
   Затем — дойти до овец. До погоды в день стрижки.
   (Sic) Имя жены пастуха. (NB) Цвет ее глаз.

2. Но не берись расплетать, если сам ты ткач неискусный,
   если ты скверный портной. Пестрядь перепутанных ниток,
   корпия библиотек, ветошка университетов[2] —   10
   кому, Любомудр, это нужно? Прежнюю пряжу сотки.
   Прежний плащ возврати той, что продрогла в углу.

2.1 Есть коллеги, что в наших (см. выше) делах неискусны.
    Все, что умеют, — кричать: «Ах, вот нарядное платье!
    Английское сукнецо! Модный русский покрой!»[3]   15

2.2 Есть и другие. Они на платье даже не взглянут.
    Все, что умеют, — считать миллиметры, чертить пунктиры.
    Выкроек вороха для них дороже, чем ткань[4].

2.3 Есть и другие. Они на государственной службе[4].
    Все, что умеют, — сличать данный наряд с униформой.   20
    Лишний фестончик найдут или карман потайной,
    тут уж портняжка держись — выговор, карцер, расстрел.

Cloth
doctoral dissertation

1. *Text* means *cloth*.[1] The rag of text is to be unwoven thread by thread.
   One must analyze the colors, catching each nuance.
   Thereafter one must explain in what color each thread is stained.
   There then follows a discussion of the weave of the cloth:
   the operation of the spindle, the deftness of the old woman's fingers.   5
   Then onto the sheep in question. The weather on shearing day.
   (Sic) The name of the shepherd's wife. (NB) The color of her eyes.

2. But don't presume to unweave if you yourself are an unskilled weaver,
   if you're a lousy tailor. Sackcloth of entangled threads,
   the lint of libraries, the rags of universities[2]—   10
   who, Philosopher, needs them? Weave the old yarn.
   Return the old mackinaw to the girl who's shivering in the corner.

2.1 There are colleagues who lack skill (see above) in our profession.
   All they can do is exclaim: "Ah, what an elegant dress!
   English burlap! A stylish Russian cut!"[3]   15

2.2 Then there are others. They won't even glance at the dress.
   All they can do is count millimeters, draw dotted lines.
   Piles of patterns are more important to them than the cloth.[4]

2.3 And there are others. They are in government service.[4]
   All they can do is check attire against the uniform.   20
   They'll find extra scallops or a hidden pocket, and
   grab the hack at once: reprimand, lockup, execution.

3. *Текст* — это *жизнь*. И ткачи его ткут. Но вбегает кондратий⁵ — и недоткал. Или ткань подверглась воздействию солнца, снега, ветра, дождя, радиации, злобы, химчистки, времени, т.е. «дни расплетают тряпочку, подаренную Тобою»⁶, и остается дыра.

3.1 Как, Любомудр, прохудилась пелена тонкотканой культуры. Лезет из каждой дыры паховитый хаос и срам⁷.

4. *Ткань* — это *текст*, это *жизнь*. Если ты доктор — дотки.

Примечания

1. См. латинский словарь. Ср. имя бабушки Гете.
2. Ср. то, что Набоков назвал «летейская библиотека».
3. Этих зову «дурачки» (см. протопоп Аввакум).
4. Ср. ср. ср. ср. ср. ср.
5. (…) Иванович (1937 — ?).
6. Бродский. Также ср. Пушкин о «рубище» и «певце», что, вероятно, восходит к Горацию: *purpureus pannus*.
7. См. см. см. см. см. см. см.!

3. *Text* is *life*. And weavers weave it. But the Reaper[5] rushes in—
and it's unfinished. Or the cloth underwent the influence
of sun, snow, wind, rain, radiation, malice, dry-cleaning, 25
time, i.e., "the days unravel the rag that You've been given,"[6]
and a hole remains.

3.1 That is how, Philosopher, the shroud of finely-woven culture wore thin.
Out of every hole crawls inguinal chaos and shame.[7]

4. *Cloth* is *text*, is *life*. If you're a doctor, sew it up. 30

Notes

1. Vide Latin dictionary. Cf. name of Goethe's grandmother.
2. Cf. what Nabokov called "the Lethean library".
3. These I call "fools" (Cf. Archpriest Avvakum).
4. Cf. Cf. Cf. Cf. Cf. Cf.
5. (. . .) Ivanovich (1937–?).
6. Brodsky. Cf. also Pushkin on "tatters" and "singer," which probably goes back to Horace: *purpureus pannus*.
7. Vide, vide, vide, vide, vide, vide!

ОТКРЫТКА ИЗ НОВОЙ АНГЛИИ. 1

Иосифу

Студенты, мыча и бодаясь, спускаются к водопою,
отплясал пять часов бубенчик на шее библиотеки,
напевая, как видишь, мотивчик, сочиненный тобою,
я спускаюсь к своей телеге.

Распускаю ворот, ремень, английские мысли,
разбредаются мои инвалиды недружным скопом.
Водобоязненный бедный Евгений (опять не умылся!)
припадает на ударную ногу, страдая четырехстопьем.

Родион во дворе у старухи-профессорши колет дровишки
(нынче время такое, что все переходят опять на печное),
и порядком оржавевший мой Холстомер, норовивший
перейти на галоп, оторжал и отправлен в ночное.

Вижу, старый да малый, пастухи костерок разжигают,
существительный хворост с одного возжигают глагола,
и томит мое сердце и взгляд разжижает,
оползая с холмов, горбуновая тень Горчакова.

Таково мы живем, таково наши дни коротая,
итальянские дядьки, Карл Иванычи, Пнины, калеки.
Таковы наши дни и труды. Таковы караваи
мы печем. То ли дело коллеги.

Вдоль реки Гераклит Ph. D. выдает брандылясы,
и трусца выдает, и трусца выдает бедолагу,
как он трусит, сердечный, как охота ему адидасы,
обогнавши поток, еще раз окунуть в ту же влагу.

Postcard from New England. 1

for Joseph

The students, lowing and butting, descend to the water trough,
the bells on the library's neck have danced off 5 o'clock,
humming, as you see, a little motif composed by you,
I go down to my wagon.

I let out my collar, my belt, and my English thoughts,
my invalids, disperse in an unruly bunch.
Hydrophobic poor Evgeny (once again forget to wash up!),
limps a bit on the stressed foot, suffering from tetrameter.

Rodion is chopping wood in the professor emerita's yard
(in times like these, everyone's going back to stoves),
and my rather rusted Kholstomer, with failing aspirations
of a gallop, neighed once and was pastured for the night.

I see shepherds, young and old alike, are kindling a campfire,
they light up the substantive brushwood from one verb,
and, crawling down from the hills, the hunchbacked
shade of Gorchakov burdens my heart and dilutes my view.

This is how we live, how our days revolve,
Italian tutors, Karl Ivaniches, Pnins, cripples.
Such are our days and works, such the cottage loaves
we bake. Our colleagues are a different matter altogether.

Along the river Heraclitus, Ph.D., weaves zigzags,
and his jog betrays, his jog betrays the poor devil,
how he's afraid, poor dear, how he yearns to outrun the stream,
to dip his Adidases once again into the same water.

А у нас накопилось довольно в крови стеарина —
понаделать свечей на февральскую ночку бы сталось.
От хорея зверея, бедной юности нашей Арина
с той же кружкой сивушною, Родионовна, бедная старость.

Я воздвиг монумент как насест этой дряхлой голубке.
– Что, осталось вина?
И она отвечает: — Вестимо-с.
До свиданья, Иосиф. Если вырвешься из мясорубки,
будешь в наших краях, обязательно навести нас.

Л.

P.S.
Генеральша Дроздова здорова. Даже спала опухоль с ног
(а то, помнишь, были, как бревна).
И в восторге Варвара Петровна —
из Швейцарий вернулся сынок.

Л.

But we've already accumulated enough stearin in our blood,
enough to make all the candles for the February night.
Brutalized by a trochee, Arina of our poor youth
with the same mug of fusel oil, Rodionovna, poor old age.

I've raised up a monument as a perch to this decrepit dove.
—Hey, any wine left?
And she answers: of course.
Goodbye, Joseph. If you get yourself out of the meat grinder
and make it out to our parts, definitely stop by.

L.

P.S.
Generalissima Drozdova is well. Even the swelling left her legs
(you remember, they were like tree trunks).
And Varvara Petrovna is in ecstasy:
her son returned from Switzerland.

L.

СТИХИ О РОМАНЕ

I

Знаем эти толстовские штучки:
с бородою, окованной льдом,
из недельной московской отлучки
воротиться в нетопленый дом.
«Затопите камин в кабинете.
Вороному задайте пшена.
Принесите мне рюмку вина.
Разбудите меня на рассвете».
Погляжу на морозный туман
и засяду за длинный роман.

Будет холодно в этом романе,
будут главы кончаться «как вдруг»,
будет кто-то сидеть на диване
и посасывать длинный чубук,
будут ели стоять угловаты,
как стоят мужики на дворе,
и, как мост, небольшое тире
свяжет две недалекие даты
в эпилоге (когда старики
на кладбище придут у реки).

Достоевский еще молоденек,
только в нем что-то есть, что-то есть.
«Мало денег, — кричит, — мало денег.
Выиграть тысяч бы пять или шесть.
Мы заплатим долги, и в итоге
будет водка, цыгане, икра.
Ах, какая начнется игра!»
После старец нам бухнется в ноги
и прочтет в наших робких сердцах
слово СТРАХ, слово КРАХ, слово ПРАХ.

Verses on the Novel

I

We know these Tolstoyan tidbits:
with a beard fettered in ice,
from a week's unexcused absence in Moscow
he returns to an unheated home.
"Light a fire in the study.
Give the black horse some millet.
Bring me a glass of wine.
Wake me at dawn."
I'll have a look at the freezing mist
and then settle into a long novel.

It will be cold in this novel,
there'll be chapters that conclude "when suddenly,"
someone will sit on a divan
and will draw on a long chibouk,
fir trees will stand about awkwardly,
like peasants in a courtyard.
And, like a bridge, a small dash
will join two neighboring dates
in the epilogue (when the old parents
arrive at the graveyard by the river).

Dostoevsky is still a youngster,
but there's something to him, something there.
"Not much money," he yells, "Not much money.
If only I can win five or six thousand.
We'll pay off the debts, and there'll be enough
left over for vodka, gypsies, and caviar.
Ah, and what a game there'll be!"
Later the elder will fall down at our feet
and will read in our timid hearts
the word FEAR, the word FAILURE, the word DUST.

Грусть-тоска. «Пой, Агаша. Пей, Саша.
Хорошо, что под сердцем сосет...»
Только нас описанье пейзажа
от такого запоя спасет.
«Красный шар догорал за лесами,
и крепчал, безусловно, мороз,
но овес на окошке пророс...»
Ничего, мы и сами с усами.
Нас не схимник спасет, нелюдим,
лучше в зеркало мы поглядим.

II

Я неизменный Карл Иваныч.
Я ваших чад целую на ночь.
Их географии учу.
Порой, одышлив и неряшлив,
я вас бужу, в ночи закашляв,
молясь и дуя на свечу.

Конечно, не большая птица,
но я имею чем гордиться:
я не блудил, не лгал, не крал,
не убивал — помилуй Боже, —
я не убийца, нет, но все же,
ах, что же ты краснеешь, Карл?

Был в нашем крае некто Шиллер,
он талер у меня зажилил.
Была дуэль. Тюрьма. Побег.
Забыв о Шиллере проклятом,
verfluchtes Fatum — стал солдатом —
сражений дым и гром побед.

Sadness-anguish. "Pour one, Agasha. Sing one, Sasha.
It's good, that there's a sucking beneath the heart . . ."
Only the landscape descriptions will save us
from such a drinking binge.
"The scarlet globe was burning low beyond the woods
and the frost had definitely gotten sharper,
but the oats in the window have sprouted . . ."
Doesn't matter, we weren't born yesterday, after all.
A schema monk, the loner, won't save us,
It's better if we take a look in the mirror.

II

I am the devoted Karl Ivanich.
I kiss your progeny goodnight.
I teach them geography.
Now and then, dishevelled and short of breath,
coughing in the night, praying and
breathing on the candle, I wake you.

Of course, I'm nobody special,
but I've a thing or two to be proud of:
I've never lechered, lied, nor stolen,
nor murdered—Lord have mercy—
I'm no murderer, but all the same,
ah, why are you blushing, Karl?

There was a certain Schiller round our way,
he touched me for a thaler, never paid it back.
There was a duel. Jail. Escape.
I forgot about the damned Schiller,
verfluchtes Fatum—became a soldier—
the smoke of battles and the thunder of victories.

Там пели, там «ура» вопили,
под липами там пиво пили,
там клали в пряники имбирь.
А здесь, как печень от цирроза,
разбухли бревна от мороза,
на окнах вечная Сибирь.

Гуляет ветер по подклетям.
На именины вашим детям
я клею домик (ни кола
ты не имеешь, старый комик,
и сам не прочь бы в этот домик).
Прошу, взгляните, Nicolas.

Мы внутрь картона вставим свечку
и осторожно чиркнем спичку,
и окон нежная слюда
засветится тепло и смутно,
уютно станет и гемютно,
и это важно, господа!

О, я привью германский гений
к стволам российских сих растений.
Фольга сияет наобум.
Как это славно и толково,
кажись, и младший понял, Лева,
хоть увалень и тугодум.

Back there they sang, they howled "Hoorah,"
and drank beer under the linden trees,
back there they put ginger in the cakes.
But here, like a liver with cirrhosis
the logs swell up from the cold,
eternal Siberia at the windows.

The wind is strolling among the cellars.
For your children's name days
I'm building a toy house (since you
don't have a thing, you old hack,
you yourself could use this house).
So please look this way, Nicolas.

We'll set a candle inside the carton
and carefully strike a match,
and the delicate mica of the windows
will light up warmly and dimly,
it will be cozy and gemuetesy,
and that's important, ladies and gentlemen!

O, I'll graft the Germanic genius
onto the stems of these Russian plants.
The tin foil flashes at random,
how splendid and clear it is;
it seems even the youngster, Lyova, understood,
although he's clumsy and doltish.

ПБГ*

Далеко, в Стране Негодяев
и неясных, но страстных знаков,
жили-были Шестов, Бердяев,
Розанов, Гершензон и Булгаков.
  Бородою в античных сплетнях,
  верещал о вещах последних

Вячеслав. Голосок доносился
до мохнатых ушей Гершензона:
«Маловато дионисийства,
буйства, эроса, пляски, озона.
  Пыль Палермо в нашем закате».
  (Пьяный Блок отдыхал на Кате,

и, достав медальон украдкой,
воздыхал Кузмин, привереда,
над беспомощной русой прядкой
с мускулистой груди правоведа,
  а Бурлюк гулял по столице,
  как утюг, и с брюквой в петлице.)

---

* Петербург, т. е. зашифрованный герой «*Поэма Без Героя*» Ахматовой.

PBG*

Far away, in the Land of Scoundrels
and obscure, yet passionate symbols,
there once lived Shestov, Berdyaev,
Rozanov, Gershenzon, and Bulgakov.
        Up to his beard in classical gossip
        Vyacheslav would be squealing

about the latest pieces. His little voice
reached the shaggy ears of Gershenzon:
"There's too little Dionysianism,
abandon, Eros, folk dance and ozone.
        The dust of Palermo is in our sunset."
        (Blok, drunk, was relaxing on Katya,

and, after furtively removing a locket,
precious Kuzmin sighed languidly
with the muscular chest of a jurist
above the helpless chestnut lock of hair,
        while Burliuk strolled about the capital,
        with a flatiron's look, and a burly boutonnière.)

---

* Petersburg, the encoded hero of Akhmatova's "Poem without a Hero," in Russian "*Poema bez geroia*".

Да, в закате над градом Петровым
рыжеватая примесь Мессины,
и под этим багровым покровом
собираются красные силы,
    и во всем недостача, нехватка:
    с мостовых исчезает брусчатка,
    чаю спросишь в трактире — несладко,
    в «Речи» что ни строка — опечатка,
    и вина не купить без осадка,
    и трамвай не ходит, двадцатка,
    и трава выползает из трещин
    силлурийского тротуара.
    Но еще это сонмище женщин
    и мужчин пило, флиртовало,
        а за столиком, рядом с эсером,
        Мандельштам волхвовал над эклером.

А эсер глядел деловито,
как босая танцорка скакала,
и витал запашок динамита
над прелестной чашкой какао.

Yes, the sunset above the Petrine city
takes on the russet hue of Messina,
and under this crimson pall
red forces are gathering,
>and there're shortages and cutbacks of everything:
>cobblestones are vanishing from the streets,
>you ask for some tea in an inn—no sugar,
>in *Speech* there's not a line without a typo,
>you can't buy wine without sediment,
>the tram isn't running, the number twenty,
>the grass is growing out of the cracks
>in the Silurian pavement.
>But still this throng of men and women
>were drinking and flirting,
>>while behind a table, next to an SR,
>>Mandel'shtam was practicing sorcery on an éclair.

And the SR looked on, businesslike,
as the barefoot dancer leapt about,
and the faint smell of dynamite
hovered over his delightful cup of cocoa.

ПУШКИНСКИЕ МЕСТА

День, вечер, одеванье, раздеванье —
всё на виду.
Где назначались тайные свиданья —
в лесу? в саду?
Под кустиком в виду мышиной норки?
à la gitane?
В коляске, натянув на окна шторки?
но как же там?
Как многолюден этот край пустынный!
Укрылся — глядь,
в саду мужик гуляет с хворостиной,
на речке бабы заняты холстиной,
голубка дряхлая с утра торчит в гостиной,
не дремлет, блядь.
О где найти пределы потаенны
на день? на ночь?
Где шпильки вынуть? скинуть панталоны?
где — юбку прочь?
Где не спугнет размеренного счастья
внезапный стук
и хамская ухмылка соучастья
на рожах слуг?
Деревня, говоришь, уединенье?
Нет, брат, шалишь.
Не оттого ли чудное мгновенье
мгновенье лишь?

Pushkin Historical Sites

Day, night, dressing, undressing:
there was no privacy.
Where did they have their secret trysts:
in the woods? in the garden?
In the shrubbery, within a mouse's purview?
À la gitane?
In the barouche with the window curtains drawn down?
but really, how then?
How crowded this deserted place is!
You've escaped notice—and then lo,
in the garden a peasant strolls with a switch,
at the river the women are busy with the wash,
my decrepit darling nanny has been lingering
in the parlor since morning, ever watchful, the whore.
O, where to find precincts hidden
for a day, for a night?
Where to pull out the hairpins? strip off the panties?
and toss the skirt?
Where will a sudden knock
and the loutish smirk of complicity
on the mugs of the servants
not frighten off my modest felicity?
The country you say, seclusion?
No, brother, you jest.
But isn't that why a wondrous moment
is merely a moment?

* * *

Грамматика есть бог ума.
Решает все за нас сама:
что проорем, а что прошепчем.
И времена пошли писать,
и будущее лезет вспять
и долго возится в прошедшем.

Глаголов русских толкотня
вконец заторкала меня,
и, рот внезапно открывая,
я знаю: не сдержать узду,
и сам не без сомненья жду,
куда-то вывезет кривая.

На перегное душ и книг
сам по себе живет язык,
и он переживет столетья.
В нем нашего — всего лишь вздох,
какой-то ах, какой-то ох,
два-три случайных междометья.

*   *   *

Grammar is indeed the god of the mind.
It alone decides all things for us:
what we will yell and what we will whisper.
And the tenses one may write,
the future crawls backwards
and slowly potters into the past.

The throng of Russian verbs
tugs at me as my grip finally loosens,
and, opening my mouth suddenly,
I know I've lost the bridle,
and, not without doubt, I wait
to see how things turn out.

Language lives independently
on the humus of souls and books,
and it will survive centuries.
In it all that remains of our own is
a sigh, an "ah," an "oh,"
two or three incidental interjections.

КЛАССИЧЕСКОЕ

В доме отдыха имени Фавна,
недалече от входа в Аид,
даже время не движется плавно,
а спокойно на месте стоит.

Зимний полдень. Начищен паркет.
Мягкий свет. Отдыхающих нет.

Полыхает в камине полено,
и тихонько туда и сюда
колыхаются два гобелена.
И на левом — картина труда:

жнут жнецы и ваятель ваяет,
жрут жрецы, Танька ваньку валяет.

А на правом, другом, гобелене
что-то выткано наоборот:
там, на фоне покоя и лени,
я на камне сижу у ворот,

без штанов, только в длинной рубашке,
и к ногам моим жмутся барашки.

«Разберемся в проклятых вопросах,
возбуждают они интерес», —
говорит, опираясь на посох,
мне нетрезвый философ Фалес.

И, с Фалесом на равной ноге,
я ему отвечаю: «Эге».

Это слово — стежок в разговоре,
так иголку втыкают в шитье.
Вот откуда Эгейское море
получило названье свое.

Classical

In the holiday home "Pan,"
not far from the entrance to Hades,
even time does not pass smoothly by,
but peacefully remains in its place.

A winter noon. The parquet just cleaned.
A soft light. No vacationers.

A log blazes in the hearth,
and two Gobelins gently
sway to and fro.
On the left, a labor scene:

the reapers reap and a sculptor sculpts,
vicars gulp their victuals, Tan'ka clowns around.

And on the right, the other Gobelin,
something is woven backwards:
there against a background of peace and idleness,
I sit upon a rock before some gates,

without pants, in a long shirt only,
and lambs rub up against my legs.

"Let us look into the accursed questions,
they arouse interest"—
the philosopher Thales, not sober,
says to me, resting on his staff.

And, on an equal footing with Thales,
I answer him: "Ah, gee."

This word is a stitch in our conversation,
just as a needle works in embroidery.
And that's how the Aegean Sea
received its name.

ДОКУМЕНТАЛЬНОЕ

Ах, в старом фильме (в старой фильме)
в окопе бреется солдат,
вокруг другие простофили
свое беззвучное галдят,
ногами шустро ковыляют,
руками быстро ковыряют
и храбро в объектив глядят.

Там, на неведомых дорожках,
следы гаубичных батарей,
мечтающий о курьих ножках
на дрожках беженец-еврей,
там день идет таким манером
под флагом черно-бело-серым,
что с каждой серией — серей.

Там русский царь в вагоне чахнет,
играет в секу и в буру.
Там лишь порой беззвучно ахнет
шестидюймовка на юру.
Там за Ольштынской котловиной
Самсонов с деловитой миной
расстегивает кобуру.

В том мире сереньком и тихом
лежит Иван — шинель, ружье.
За ним Франсуа, страдая тиком,
в беззвучном катится пежо.
. . . .
Еще раздастся рев ужасный,
еще мы кровь увидим красной,
еще насмотримся ужо.

Documentary

Ah, in the old motion picture (moving picture)
the soldier shaves in the trench,
the others gawk about,
raising their soundless din,
nimbly hobble about,
quickly jerk their hands around,
and boldly gaze into the camera lens.

There are tracks of howitzer batteries
on the nondescript trails, and,
on a droshky sits a Jewish refugee
dreaming of chicken legs;
there, under a black-white-grey flag
the day proceeds in such a way
that it grows greyer with each week's serial.

There the Russian czar withers in his rail coach
playing card games.
Only now and then does a six-incher
silently sigh on an exposed height.
There beyond the Olsztyn basin.
Samsonov, with serious mien,
unbuttons his holster flap.

In that silent and greyish world
lies Ivan, his greatcoat and rifle.
Behind him François, suffering a tick,
drives off in his soundless Peugeot.
. . . .
A terrible howl will yet resound,
we will yet see crimson blood,
and we will surely see our fill.

ИНСТРУКЦИЯ РИСОВАЛЬЩИКУ ГЕРБОВ

1-й вариант

На фоне щита,
иль таза, иль мелкого блюда
изображение небольшого верблюда,
застрявшего крепко в игольном ушке,
при этом глядящего на кота, сидящего в черном мешке,
завязанном лентой цвета нимфы, купающейся в пруду,
по коей ленте красивым курсивом надпись:
SCRIPTA MANENT
(лат. «Не легко, но пройду»)

2-й вариант

На постаменте в виде опрокинутой стопки
две большие скобки,
к коим стоят, как бы привалившись:
справа — лось сохатый,
слева — лев пархатый;
в скобках вставший на дыбы Лифшиц;
изо рта извивается эзопов язык,
из горла вырывается зык,
хвост прищемлен, на голове лежит корона в виде кепки,
фон: лесорубы рубят лес — в Лифшица летят щепки,
в лапах и копытах путается гвардейская лента
с надписью:
ЗВЕРЕЙ НЕ КОРМИТЬ

3-й вариант (поскромнее)

Земной шар
в венце из хлебных колосьев,
перевитых лентой;
на поясках
красивым курсивом надпись:
ЛЕВ ЛОСЕВ
на 15-ти языках.

Instructions to a Heraldic Illustrator

First Version

Against the background
of a shield, or a basin, or
a shallow saucer, the rendering of
a moderately sized camel, stuck tight in
the eye of a needle, yet looking at a cat in a black
bag tied up with a flower-ribbon the color of a nymph, bathing
in a pond, upon whose ribbon, in a beautiful script, the legend reads:
SCRIPTA MANENT
(Lat. "it's not easy, but I'll make it")

Second Version

On a pedestal in the shape of an overturned drinking cup
two great parentheses
adjoining which, as if leaning against them:
on the right: an antlered moose,
on the left: a mangy lion;
In the parentheses, Lifshits up on his hind legs,
an Aesopian tongue curls out of his mouth,
a loud cry breaks out of his throat,
his tail is pinched, on his head sits a crown shaped like a cap,
the background: lumberjacks are clearing the forest, chips
are flying at Lifshits, in his paws and hooves a tangled
heraldic ribbon, with the legend:
DO NOT FEED THE ANIMALS

Third Version (a bit more modest)

The earthly globe
within a wreath of ears of grain
bound with a ribbon;
across the tropics
in a beautiful script the legend:
LEV LOSEV
in 15 languages.

* * *

Мы наблюдаем при солнца восходе
круговорот алкоголя в природе.
Полно сидеть пучеглазой совой
здесь, на плече у Паллады Афины —
где-то баллады звенят и графины,
что бы такое нам сделать с собой?

То ли тряхнуть словарем, как мошною,
то ли отделаться рифмой смешною,
то ли веревочкой горе завить?
Юмор, гармония, воображенье,
выходки водки и пива броженье,
жажда и жар, и желанье запить —

как это в сущности все изоморфно!
Пташка пропела свое и замолкла.
Пташечка! Ты не одна ли из тех
неисчислимых вчерашних рюмашек,
как эта скатерть июньских ромашек
в пятнах коньячных вчерашних утех.

Знаю, когда отключимся с похмелья,
нас, забулдыг, запихнут в подземелье,
так утрамбуют, что будь здоров.
Там уж рассыплемся, там протрезвеем.
Только созреем опять и прозреем
для бесконечных грядущих пиров.

* * *

With the rising of the sun we observe
the alcohol cycle in nature.
Enough sitting like a wide-eyed owl
here on the shoulder of Pallas Athena:
somewhere ballads and carafes are ringing,
so what shall we do with ourselves?

Shall we throw words around as though they were money,
shall we get off lightly with a comic rhyme,
shall we pack up our troubles?
Humor, harmony, imagination,
the outbursts of vodka and the fermentation of beer,
thirst and swelter and the desire to drink—

how essentially isomorphous it all is!
The early bird sang its tune and was silent.
Sweet bird! Are you not one of those
innumerable wineglasses from last night,
like this table cloth of June camomiles
with the brandy stains of last night's fun?

I know, when we pass out from drinking,
they'll stuff us prodigal ones in the dungeon,
and tramp us down so well, you better watch out!
Then we'll go to pieces, then we'll sober up.
Only we'll ripen again and see the light
for the endless coming feasts.

* * *
1.

Земную жизнь пройдя до середины,
я был доставлен в длинный коридор.
В нелепом платье бледные мужчины

вели какой-то смутный разговор.
Стучали кости. Испускались газы,
и в воздухе подвешенный топор

угрюмо обрубал слова и фразы:
все ху да ху, да е мае, да бля —
печальны были грешников рассказы.

Один заметил, что за три рубля
сегодня ночью он кому-то вдует,
но некто, грудь мохнатую скобля,

ему сказал, что не рекомендует,
а третий, с искривленной головой,
воскликнул, чтоб окно закрыли — дует.

В ответ ему раздался гнусный вой,
развратный, негодующий, унылый,
но в грязных робах тут вошел конвой,

и я был унесен нечистой силой.
Наморща лобик, я лежал в углу.
Несло мочой, карболкой и могилой.

В меня втыкали толстую иглу,
меня поили горечью полынной.
К холодному железному столу

потом меня доской прижали длинной,
и было мне дышать запрещено
во мраке этой комнаты пустынной.

* * *

1.

Midway in the journey of my earthly life
I found myself in a long corridor.
Pale men in awkward smocks

were talking about something obscure.
Bones were knocking together. Gasses were being released,
an axe suspended in midair

sullenly lopped off words and phrases:
It's a fu ing lo of sh , uck it all—
sad were the tales of the sinners.

One remarked that for three rubles
tonight he would blow someone,
but another, scraping his hairy chest,

told him he didn't recommend it,
while the third, his head bent round,
yelled to shut the window, there's a draft.

In answer a vile wail rang out,
depraved, indignant, doleful,
but then an escort in filthy robes entered,

and I was carried off by the unclean force.
With furrowed brow, I lay down in the corner.
It reeked of urine, disinfectant, and the grave.

They drove a thick needle into me,
and gave me a bitter absinthe to drink.
Then they pressed me with a long board

against a cold iron table
and I was forbidden to breathe
in the gloom of that empty room.

И хриплый голос произнес: «Кино».
В ответ визгливый: «Любоваться нечем».
А тот: «Возьми и сердце заодно».

А та: «Сейчас, сперва закончу печень».
И мой фосфоресцировал скелет,
обломан, обезличен, обесцвечен,

корявый остов тридцати трех лет.

2.

От этого, должно быть, меж ресниц
такая образовывалась линза,
что девушка дрожала в ней, и шприц,

как червячок, и рос и шевелился.
Вытягивалась кверху, как свеча,
и вниз катилась, горяча, больница.

(То, что коснулось левого плеча,
напоминало птицу или ветку,
толчок звезды, зачатие луча,

укол крыла, проклюнувшего клетку,
пославший самописку ЭКГ
и вкривь и вкось перекарябать сетку

миллиметровки.) Голос: «Эк его».
Другой в ответ: «Взгляни на пот ладоней».
Они звучали плохо, роково,

но, вместе с тем, все глуше, отдаленней,
уже и вовсе слышные едва,
не разберешь, чего они долдонят.

Я возлетал. Кружилась голова.
Мелькали облака, неуследимы.
И я впервые обретал слова,

земную жизнь пройдя до середины.

And a hoarse voice said, "the movies".
A shrill one responded, "nothing good's playing."
And the first: "Get his heart at the same time."

And she: "Just a minute, I'm finishing the liver."
And my skeleton was phosphorescent,
disjointed, depersonalized, decolored,

a gnarled frame of thirty-three years.

   2.

That is probably why between my eyelashes
there appeared such a lens,
that the nurse shimmered in it, and the syringe,

like a little worm, grew and began to stir.
The hospital, inflamed, shot upward,
like a candle, then rushed downward.

(What touched my left shoulder
reminded me of a bird or twig,
the shove of a star, the conception of a ray,

the thrust of a wing, pecked through the cage
and made the recording pen of the EKG
jerk all over the millimeter-lined

scale.) A voice: "Oh, look at that."
Another answers: "Take a look at the sweaty palms."
They sounded serious, ominous,

yet at the same time also fainter, more distant,
soon hardly audible anymore, you
couldn't tell what they were babbling about.

I flew up. My head was spinning.
Clouds whisked by, at once lost to the eye,
and for the first time I found words,

midway in the journey of my life.

3.

Ты что же так забрался высоко,
Отец? Сияет имя на табличке:
«…в чьем ведении Земля, Вода и К° …»

И что еще? Не разберу без спички.
День изо дня. Да, да. День изо дня
Ты крошишь нам, а мы клюем, как птички.

Я знаю, что не стребуешь с меня
Долгов (как я не вспомню ведь про трешку,
Что занял друг), не бросишь, отгоня

Пустого гостя. Просит на дорожку
Хоть посошок … Вот черт! Куда ни кинь…
За эту бесконечную матрешку,

Где в Царстве Сила, в Силе Слава…

3.

Why'd you climb all the way up here,
Father? the name plate shines:
". . . under whose jurisdiction the Earth, Water, and Co. . . ."

And what else? I can't make it out without a match.
Day after day. Yes, yes. Day after day
you toss us crumbs and we peck at them, like birds.

I'm sure you won't call in any of my debts
(just like I forgo that fiver
my friend borrowed), you won't chase out

a thirsty guest. How about just a quick
one for the road . . . Damn it! Wherever you look...
for this endless matroshka,

Where in the Kingdom is Power, and in Power is Glory. . .

УРОК ФОТОГРАФИИ

Photography Lesson

МОСКВИЧИ

1.

Дворовая свора бежала куда-то.
Визжала девчонка одна.
«Я их де-фло-ри-ру-ю пиццикато», —
промолвил старик у окна.

Он врал и осекся, трепач этот древний,
московской орды старожил.
Он в комнату выплывшей Анне Андреевне
услужливо стул предложил.

Он к ней обращался с почтительным креном,
он чайничек ей подержал.
Его, побывавший в корзиночке с кремом,
мизинец при этом дрожал.

Он маялся, мальчик шестидесятилетний,
но все же отважился на
рассказ, начиненный последнею сплетней,
и слух не замкнула она.

Он даже заставил ее улыбнуться,
он все-таки ей угодил,
москвич, отдуватель чаинок на блюдце,
писатель стишков в «Крокодил».

Muscovites

1.

The watchdogs were running somewhere.
A solitary girl squealed.
"I'll de-flo- them pizzicato,"
said the old man at the window.

He was lying and stopped short, that ancient
blatherer, remnant of the Muscovite horde.
He courteously offered a chair
to Anna Andreevna as she sailed into the room.

He listed towards her deferentially,
and held the delicate teapot for her.
His little finger quivered all the same,
recently removed from the cream pitcher.

He was suffering, that sixty-year old boy,
but nevertheless ventured
a story, crammed with the latest gossip,
and she didn't close her ears.

He even made her laugh,
he pleased her after all, he,
the Muscovite, scourge of tealeaves and saucers,
writer of verses in *Crocodile*.

2.

Поникла, чай, моя камелия,
а ежели еще жива,
знать, из метели и похмелья
сидит и вяжет кружева.

Окно черно в вечерних шторах,
там, в аввакумовых просторах,
морозный вакуум и тьма
ей выдается задарма.

Итак, она не растеряла
ни мастерства, ни материала,
в привычных пальцах вьется нить,
ловка пустóты обводить.

Сидит, порою дурь глотает,
и пустоты́ кругом хватает,
да уменьшается клубок.
И мрак за окнами глубок.

2.

My camellia, most probably, has wilted,
and if she's still alive,
it seems, she sits and embroiders
lace out of the blizzard and hangover.

The window is black against the evening blinds,
there, in the Avvakumian expanses
the frozen vacuum and darkness
tempt her attention in vain.

And so, she lost neither her skill
nor her material, in her
accustomed fingers the thread twists,
to deftly outline the emptinesses.

She sits, at times swallowing foolishness,
and there is plenty of emptiness around,
may the ball grow smaller.
And the dark beyond the windows is deep.

3.

Любви, надежды, черта в стуле
недолго тешил нас уют.
Какие книги издаются в Туле!
В Америке таких не издают.

Чу! проскакало крошечное что-то
в той стороне, где теплится душа.
Какая тонкая работа!
Шедевр косого алкаша.

Ах! В сердце самое куснула.
И старый черт таращится со стула,
себе слезы не извиня:
что это — проскочило, промелькнуло,
булатными подковками звеня?

3.

We weren't entertained for long by
the comfort of love, hope and the devil in the chair.
What books are published in Tula!
They don't publish books like that in America.

Hark! something tiny galloped past
on that side, where the soul glimmers.
What refined workmanship!
A chef-d'oeuvre of a cross-eyed drunk.

Ah, it touched me to the quick.
And the old devil gawks from his chair
and doesn't grudge himself his tears:
what is it that rushed past, flashed out of sight,
with the ringing of damask horseshoes?

АМФИБРОНХИТНАЯ НОЧЬ

1. Газета на ночь

Андроповская старуха
лобзнула казенный гранит,
и вот уже новая муха
кремлевскую стену чернит.
Деды́ — да которым бы в баньке
попарить остаток костей,
которым бы внучке бы, Таньке,
подсовывать жменю сластей,
которым бы ночью в исподнем
на печке трещать с требухи,
которым бы в храме Господнем
замаливать горько грехи,
чего-то бормочут, натужась,
то лапку о лапку помнут,
то ножками выдадут ужас
считаемых ими минут.
Тоска в этих бывших мужчинах,
пугливых, гугнивых дедах,
в их мелких повадках мушиных,
в их черных мушиных следах.
Прости им, Господь, многоточья,
помилуй трухлявый их ряд.
Уж эти не ведают точно.
Да, собственно, и не творят.

Amphibronchic Night

1. Evening Paper

Andropov's old lady
kissed the official granite
and already a new fly
blackens the Kremlin wall.
They're grandpas—who should be
steaming what's left of their bones in a bathhouse,
who should be shoving a fistful of sweets
at their granddaughter, Tanka,
who at night should be lying, with creaking guts,
in their underclothes on the stove,
who in the Lord's church should
atone bitterly for their sins—
instead, they mutter something, tense with effort,
first rubbing paw on paw, then
their nervous feet betraying
the suffering of those minutes they count off.
There is something melancholy about these quondam men,
these timorous grandpas who speak through their noses
in their petty fly-like habits.
Forgive them, Lord, their omission points,
have mercy on their moldering ranks.
Already they don't have their full wits anymore
and, strictly speaking, they don't do anything.

2. Старый сон

Знать, не у природы на лоне,
знать, в химкомбинатском бору
добыты те шкурки нейлоньи.
Напяливши эту муру,
в трамвае толпа непреклонней
сжимает (похоже — умру).

Последних песцов поколенье
покоится на Соловках,
а этих окраска — гиенья,
вся в пятнышках и волосках.
И явственней запах гниенья —
до яростной боли в висках.

Трамвай шёл какой-то там номер.
Ламца-дрицаца-дрицаца.
Не я ль на площадочке помер?
Тащите меня, мертвеца.
Лица так никто и не повер-
нул — нуль был на месте лица —

склоняют подобия пяток
над мелкой печатью страниц,
в портфелях котлетовый взяток
и робкий десяток яиц,
за окнами мокрый остаток
деления школ и больниц.

Расправить покорные власти
немытые трубочки шей?
Взглянуть хоть на новый фаланстер
в 14 этажей?
Но гаркнул водитель: «Вылазьте,
приехали…»

2. An Old Dream

It seems these nylon hides were won
not in the heart of nature, but
rather in the wilds of a chemical plant.
Wedged into this stuff,
the crowd in the tram presses
more inflexibly (I believe I'm dying).

The generation of the latest fox furs
lies fallen at Solovki,
whereas these have a hyena's coloration,
all flecks and hair.
The distinct odor of rotting too,
which brings a frenzied pain to the temples.

Some number tram ran by there.
Purdy-thurdy-thurdy.
Did I die at the stop?
Take me away, a dead man.
Nobody even turned their face
—nothing instead of a face—

Looking similar to feet they
hunch over the small print of their pages,
in their briefcases a catch of pork chops,
and a dozen timid eggs,
past the window the damp remainder
of the division of schools and hospitals.

To straighten out the unwashed tubes
of their necks, obedient to power?
To take a look at the new 14-story
phalanstery?
But the driver barked out: "Scram,
we've arrived . . ."

3. Ante Lucem

Я что — в каждой бочке затычка?
мне тоже бывает невмочь.
Но вижу, проставлена √
в графе «пережить эту ночь».

А может быть, сердце из клетки
грудной улетело в окно,
чирикает, сидя на ветке,
мол, холодно, страшно, темно.

Но вот уж светать начинает.
Вот солнце встает над стрехой
и утра пирог начиняет
своей золотой чепухой.

3. Ante Lucem

What can I do?—has every keg got a plug?
Sometimes I too can't take it anymore.
But I see a √ written in
the column "survives this night."

Or, perhaps my heart flew out
of my rib cage and out the window
and twitters, perched on a branch,
to say that it's cold, frightening, and dark.

But dawn is already breaking.
The sun is rising above the eaves
and stuffing the tart of the day
with its golden nonsense.

РАЗГОВОР

«Нас гонят от этапа до этапа,
А Польше в руки все само идет —
Валенса, Милош, Солидарность, Папа,
у нас же Солженицын, да и тот
Угрюм-Бурчеев и довольно средний
прозаик». «Нонсенс, просто он последний
романтик». «Да, но если вычесть "ром"».
«Ну, ладно, что мы все-таки берем?»
Из омута лубянок и бутырок
приятели в коммерческий уют
всплывают, в яркий мир больших бутылок.
«А пробовал ты шведский "Абсолют",
его я называю "соловьевка",
шарахнешь — и София тут как тут».
«А все же затрапезная столовка,
где под столом гуляет поллитровка …
нет, все-таки, как белая головка,
так западные водки не берут».
«Прекрасно! ностальгия по сивухе!
А по чему еще — по стукачам?
по старым шлюхам, разносящим слухи?
по слушанью "Свободы" по ночам?
по жакту? по райкому? по погрому?
по стенгазете "За культурный быт"?»
«А может, нам и правда выпить рому —
уж этот точно свалит нас с копыт».

Conversation

"They hound us at every stage
but Poland sets its own course,
Walesa, Milosz, Solidarnost, the Pope,
sure we have Solzhenitsyn, also that
gloom-and-doomer, a rather pedestrian
prose stylist." "Nonsense, he's simply
the last romantic." "Fine, if you subtract the 'rom-'."
"OK, ok, what shall we have anyway?"
Out of the whirlpool of Lubyankas and Butyrkas
friends surfaced into the free-market refuge,
into the vivid world of big bottles.
"But have you tried the Swedish 'Absolut,'
I call it 'Solovyovka,'
one shot, and there's Sophia right there."
"But, all the same, the lunches at work,
where a half-liter wanders under the table . . .
no, nonetheless, white top,
the western vodkas can't beat it."
"That's great! homesick for rockgut!
for what else: informers?
for old hookers who spread rumors?
for listening to "Liberty" at night?
the farm combine? the district party committee? the pogrom?
for the wall-newspaper *Cultural Living* ?"
"Maybe we really should drink to rum:
that alone will knock us off our hooves."

ПИСЬМО НА РОДИНУ

*Как ваши руки, Молли, погрубели,
как опустился ваш веселый Дик...*
Кузмин, "Переселенцы"

Дали нары. Дали вилы. Навоз
ковырять нелегко,
но жратвы от пуза.
С тех пор, как выехали из Союза,
воды не пьем — одно молоко.
По субботам — от бешеной коровки
(возгонка, какая не снилась в Москве).
Доллареску откладываем в коробки
из-под яиц. У меня уже две.
Хозяева, ну, не страшнее овира,
конечно, дерьмо, но я их факу.
Франц — тюфяк, его Эльзевира –
мразь, размазанная по тюфяку.
Очень дешевы куры. Овощи
в ассортименте. Фрукты — всегда.
Конечно, некоторые, как кур в ощип,
попали сюда, с такими беда.
Выступал тут вчера один кулема,
один мой кореш в виде стишков,
мол, «хорошо нам на родине, дома,
в сальных ватниках с толщей стежков».
Знаем — сирень, запашок мазута,
родимый уют бессменных рубах.
А все же свобода лучше уюта,
в работниках лучше, чем в рабах.
Мы тут не морячки в загране,
а навсегда. Вот еще бы скопить
коробку… Говорят, за горами
еще не всё успели скупить.
Нам бы только для первой оснастки,
а там пусть соток хоть семь, пусть шесть.
Есть за горами еще участки.
Свободные пустоши есть.

Letter to the Old Country

> How your hands, Molly, have grown so coarse,
> how your cheerful Dick has let himself go...
> Kuzmin, "Settlers"

They provided a bunk. They provided a pitchfork.
It wasn't easy going with the manure,
but it's grub from the guts.
Since we left the Union
we don't drink water, only milk.
And on Saturdays from a rabid cow
(that's sublimation I'd never dreamed of in Moscow).
We're putting aside a few dollars in egg
cartons. I already have two.
The bosses are no worse than the passport office at home.
Of course there's crap, but I'll fuck 'em over.
Franz is a tub and his Elzevira
is the scum that grows on the tub.
The chickens are very cheap. And there's
a variety of vegetables. And always fruit.
Of course, some come over here and
get fleeced straightaway. It's a real pity.
Just last night a guy came out,
one of my buddies, with some poetry,
which went, "it's good back in the home country, at home,
in greasy vatniki with thick stitches."
We know: lilac, the scent of diesel,
the homey comfort of unchanged shirts.
But still, freedom is better than comfort.
Better to be among the workers than the slaves.
We're not sailors in a port of call here,
this is for good. Still if we can save
up another carton . . . They say that over the mountains
not everything has been bought up yet.
We'd only need enough for the initial outlay,
even if they're only seven-hundredth parts, even six.
There are still land lots on the far side of the mountains.
There're still free tracts of land.

* * *

Тем и прекрасны эти сны,
что все же доставляют почту
куда нельзя, в подвал, в подпочву,
в глубь глубины,

где червячки живут, сочась,
где прячут головы редиски,
где вы заключены сейчас
без права переписки.

Все вы, которые мертвы,
мои друзья, мои родные,
мои враги (пока живые),
ну, что же вы

смеетесь, как в немом кино.
Ведь нет тебя, ведь ты же умер,
так в чем же дело, что за юмор,
что так смешно?

Однажды, завершая сон,
я сделаю глубокий выдох
и вдруг увижу слово *выход* —
так вот где он!

Сырую соль с губы слизав,
я как вам пойду тропинкой зыбкой
и уж тогда проснусь с улыбкой,
а не в слезах.

*   *   *

And yet these dreams are beautiful,
because nonetheless they deliver mail
to impossible places, to a cellar, underground,
to the deepest depths,

where oozing worms dwell,
where radishes hide heads,
where you're now imprisoned,
without the right to correspondence.

All of you, who are now dead,
my friends, my countrymen,
my enemies (while alive),
well, why are you

laughing, as in a silent film.
For you're no more, you're dead you see,
so what's the deal, why the humor,
what's so funny?

One day, finishing a dream,
I'll heave a heavy sigh
and suddenly see the word "exit"—
so there it is!

Licking the damp salt from my lips,
I'll follow the unsteady path to you,
and then will surely wake up smiling
instead of crying.

НА РОЖДЕСТВО

Я лягу, взгляд расфокусирую,
звезду в окошке раздвою
и вдруг увижу местность сирую,
сырую родину свою.

Во власти оптика-любителя
не только что раздвой — и сдвой,
а сдвой Сатурна и Юпитера
чреват Рождественской звездой.

Вослед за этой, быстро вытекшей
и высохшей, еще скорей,
всходи над Волховом и Вытегрой
звезда волхвов, звезда царей.

. . . .

Звезда взойдет над зданьем станции,
и радио в окне сельпо
программу по заявкам с танцами
прервет растерянно и, по-
медлив малость, как замолится
о пастухах, волхвах, царях,
о коммунистах с комсомольцами,
о сброде пьяниц и нерях.
Слепцы, пророки трепотливые,
отцы, привыкшие к кресту,
как эти строки терпеливые,
бредут по белому листу.
Где розовою промокашкою
в полнеба запад возникал,
туда за их походкой тяжкою
Обводный тянется канал.
Закатом наскоро промокнуты,
слова идут к себе домой
и открывают двери в комнаты,
давно покинутые мной.

At Christmas

I'll lie down and let my eyes go out of focus,
and split in two the star in the window,
and suddenly I'll see that orphaned place,
my damp homeland.

The optics enthusiast has not only
the power of division but also of doubling,
and the doubling of Saturn and Jupiter
is pregnant with the Christmas star.

After this star, which quickly flowed out
and dried, let yet swifter
the star of the Magi, the star of czars
ascend above the Volkov and the Vytegra.

. . . .

The star will rise above the station's building
and absentmindedly interrupt the radio in
the village general store's window, in the middle
of its dance-music request program, and will
linger a little, as though to pray for
the shepherds, the Magi, and czars,
the communists with their Komsomol members,
and the rabble of drunks and bums.
Blind men, cautious prophets,
fathers, accustomed to the cross,
like these unhurried lines
will wander across the white page.
Behind their solemn gait
the Obvodny canal stretches
towards where the west was rising
into the nether-sky like pink blotting paper.
Hastily blotted by the sunset,
the words head homeward
and open doors into rooms
which I'd abandoned long ago.

* * *

С. К.

И наконец остановка «Кладбище».
Нищий, надувшийся, словно клопище,
в крутке-москвичке сидит у ворот.
Денег даю ему — он не берет.

Как же, твержу, мне поставлен в аллейке
памятник в виде стола и скамейки,
с кружкой, поллитрой, вкрутую яйцом,
следом за дедом моим и отцом.

Слушай, мы оба с тобой обнищали,
оба вернуться сюда обещали,
ты же по списку проверь, я же ваш,
ты уж пожалуйста, ты уж уважь.

Нет, говорит, тебе места в аллейке,
нету оградки бетонной бадейки,
фото в овале, сирени куста,
столбика нету и нету креста.

Словно я Мистер какой-нибудь Твистер,
не подпускает на пушечный выстрел,
под козырек, издеваясь, берет,
что ни даю — ничего не берет.

*   *   *

for S .K.

And finally, the bus stop "Cemetery."
A beggar, swollen up like a bug,
sits before the gates in a Moscovite jacket.
I offer him some money: he doesn't take it.

How is it possible, I repeat to myself, that
a monument's been raised to me in the cemetery path,
in the shape of a table and bench, with a tankard, a half-liter
and a hard-boiled egg, right behind my dad and granddad.

Listen, we both have grown poor, and
we both promised to return here, you
can certainly check the records, I'm yours alright,
but please, go right ahead and humor me.

He says, there's no room for you in the path,
there's no fence and no stone basin,
no portrait in an oval, no lilacs,
there's no column and no cross.

As if I were some kind of Mister Twister,
he doesn't let me near no matter what,
he salutes me mockingly and,
no matter what I offer, takes nothing.

* * *

Читая Милоша

Нам звуки ночные давно невдомек,
но вы замечали: всегда
в период упадка железных дорог
слышней но ночам поезда.
И вот он доносится издалека —
в подушку ль уйдешь от него.
Я книгу читал одного старика,
поляка читал одного.
Пустынный простор за окном повторял
описанный в книге простор,
и я незаметно себя потерял
в его рассужденье простом.
И вот он зачем-то уводит меня
в пещеры платоновой мрак,
где жирных животных при свете огня
рисует какой-то дурак.
И я до конца рассужденье прочел,
и выпустил книгу из рук,
и слышу — а поезд еще не прошел,
все так же доносится стук.
А мне-то казалось, полночи, никак
не меньше, провел я в пути,
но даже еще не успел товарняк
сквозь наш полустанок пройти.
Я слышу, как рельсы гудят за рекой,
и шпалы, и моста настил,
и кто-то прижал мое горло рукой
и снова его отпустил.

* * *

Reading Milosz

We'd long ago grown deaf to nocturnal sounds,
but you'd remarked: always during
the decline of the railroads, the trains
were actually more audible at night.
And it swiftly reaches you from afar,
whether you try to escape it beneath the pillow or not.
I was reading the book of an old man,
I was reading an old Pole.
The empty expanse past the window
repeated the expanse described in the book,
and, without noticing, I lost myself
in his straightforward discourse.
And then for some reason he's leading me
into the gloom of Plato's cave,
where some fool draws plump animals
by the light of a fire.
I read his argument to the end,
and let the book fall from my hands,
and I listen, but the train hasn't come by yet,
although I hear its rumble.
And it seemed to me that I spent
half the night, not a minute less, on the tracks,
but even the freight train
hasn't passed by our station yet.
I listen to the rails hum past the river,
and the sleeper cars, and the bridge's wooden slats,
and someone squeezed my throat with his hand
and let it go again.

ТРАМВАЙ

На Обводном канале,
где я детство отбыл,
мы жестянку гоняли —
называлось: футбол.
Этот звук жестяной
мне охоту отбил
к коллективной игре
под кирпичной стеной.

Блещут мутные перлы
треть столетья назад.
Извержения спермы
в протяженный мазут.
Как мешочки медуз,
по каналу ползут
эти лузы любви,
упустившие груз.

Нитяной пуповиной
в Обводный канал,
нефтяною лавиной —
на фабричный сигнал,
предрассветный гудок
подгонял, подгонял
каждый сон, каждый взгляд,
каждый чаю глоток.

Позабыт, позамучен
с молодых юных лет.
Вон в траве, замазучен,
мой трамвайный билет,
ни поднять, ни поддать
(сырость, кости болят).
Цифры: тройка, семерка.
Остальных не видать.

The Tram

At the Obvodny canal,
where I served out my childhood,
we used to chase a tin can,
and this was called "soccer."
That tin-plated sound
disinclined me from
collective sport
beside a brick wall.

The lusterless pearls of
a third of a century ago sparkle.
Spurts of sperm float
in the wake of diesel oil.
Like jelly fish sacs,
these pockets of love,
unburdened of their freight,
crawl along the canal.

Like a cotton umbilical cord
to the Obvodny canal,
like an oily avalanche—
at the factory's signal,
the predawn whistle
would chase on
every dream, every glance,
every gulp of tea.

Forgotten, and its luster faded
since those early, youthful years,
over there in the grass, smeared with oil,
lies my tram ticket.
I won't pick it up, nor kick it away
(the dampness, my bones ache).
The numbers: a three, a seven.
I can't read the others.

Этот стих меня тащит,
как набитый трамвай,
под дождем дребезжащий
над пожухлой травой;
надо мне выходить
было раньше строфой;
ничего, не беда,
посижу взаперти

со счастливым билетом
во взмокшей горсти.

This verse drags me along
like a crowded tram,
clattering in the rain
along the withered grass.
I should have gotten off
this strophe earlier;
it's alright, no harm done,
I'll lock myself away

with the lucky ticket
in my sweat-drenched fist.

МАРШ

За оркестра вздыхающей тубою
под белесой овчинкой небес,
притворившись афишною тумбою,
ветерком в подворотне, не без
холодка по спине,
наяву, как во сне,
пройти с опаской,
где пахнет краской
и стынет студень на окне.

Освещен маловаттною лампою
старый лев на столетнем посту,
под чугунной облупленной лапою
я записку найду и прочту:
«Иди туда, не знаю куда,
принеси то, не знаю что,
и аккуратно
вернись обратно
лет через десять или сто».

И пошел, и сносил свою голову
и, вернувшись, задрал высоко:
мойка окон, мелькание голого,
синька неба и синька трико,
пена плещется вниз,
вышел кот на карниз,
ужасен голод,
но вот он, голубь…
Кис-кис-кис-кис, кис-кис, кис-кис!
      (кис-кис, кис-кис!)

A March

Behind the sighing tuba of the orchestra,
beneath the sky's whitish sheepskin coat,
imitating an advertising column,
or like a gust of wind beneath the gate,
not without a chill along the spine,
wide awake, as if dreaming,
to walk gingerly past,
where it smells of paint and
meat-jelly cools on the windowsill.

The old lion at his ancient post
lit up by the low-watt lightbulb,
under the flaking cast-iron paw
I find a note and read:
"Please go I don't know where
and get I don't know what,
and, to be exact,
please come back
in about ten or a hundred years."

I set off, and didn't lose my head
and, returning, craned it high:
windows to be washed, a glimpse of a nude,
the blueing of the sky, the blueing of tricot,
and foam splashing downwards,
the cat went out on the ledge,
terribly hungry,
but there's a pigeon over there . . .
kitty-kitty-kitty, kitty-kitty!
              (kitty-kitty!)

Возле старого здания желтого
в черной шляпе и в черном пальто
с полной кружкой чего-то тяжелого
недоверчиво смотрит Никто.
Прислонился себе
к водосточной трубе,
и постепенно
хмельная пена
дрожит и тает на губе.

Дал нам Бог наконец наводнение,
град и трус, и струи дождя.
Отсырелое недоумение
проступило на морде вождя.
Лишь гвардии георгин,
Александр Александрович Басаргин,
у здания клуба,
где мокнет клумба,
с похмелья высится один
                        (совсем один!).
Вздыхает туба.
Промокла тумба.
Во всех театрах карантин.

Near the old yellow building,
in a black hat and black coat,
with a mug full of something heavy
No-one looks on skeptically.
He's leaning against a drainpipe,
and gradually
the heady froth
quivers and melts on his lip.

At last God gave us a flood,
hailstones and an earthquake, and torrents of rain.
A damp bewilderment
showed through the chief's mug.
Only the dahlia of the Guards,
Aleksandr Aleksandrovich Basargin,
at the club house
where the flower beds are soused
rises alone from the hangover
        (absolutely alone!)
The tuba is sighing.
The advertising column's drenched.
All the theatres are in quarantine.

УРОК ФОТОГРАФИИ. 1

Вот еще. Что ты плачешь, дурак?
Посмотри на картинку в кулак
и увидишь, как две спины
отделяются от стены,
обретают объем черты,
раскрывает улыбка рты,
и вперед протянулась рука,
а не знают два пиджака,
две рубашки, две головы,
что давно уж они мертвы.
Там, где груда пальто и шляп,
недодержан, как белая мышь
(видно, был проявитель слаб),
приглядись — это ты стоишь.

Я стою, прислонясь к стене,
недодержан и под хмельком,
и гляжу: грядущее мне
угловатым грозит кулаком.

Photography Lesson. 1

Here's another. What are you crying for, you fool?
Look at the picture through your fist
and you'll see two backs
separate from the wall,
and acquire the capacity of a form.
A smile uncovers the mouths,
and a hand reaches forward,
and two jackets, two shirts,
two heads don't realize
that they're long dead.
There, that heap of coats and hats,
underexposed, like a white mouse
(apparently the developer was weak),
look closely—that's you there.

I'm standing, leaning against the wall,
underexposed and tipsy,
and look: the future threatens me
with an angular fist.

* * *

«Все пряжи рассучились,
опять кудель в руке,
и люди разучились
играть на тростнике.

Мы в наши полимеры
вплетаем клок шерсти́,
но эти полумеры
не могут нас спасти...»

Так я, сосуд скудельный,
неправильный овал,
на станции Удельной
сидел и тосковал.

Мне было спрятать негде
души моей дела,
и радуга из нефти
передо мной цвела.

И столько понапортив
и понаделав дел,
я за забор напротив
бессмысленно глядел.

Дышала психбольница,
светились корпуса,
а там мелькали лица,
гуляли голоса,

там пели что придется,
переходя на крик,
и финского болотца
им отвечал тростник.

* * *

"All the threads have come undone,
again I'm left with tow in my hands,
and the people have forgotten
how to play the reed.

We weave a shred of wool
into our polymers,
but these half measures
can't save us . . ."

Thus I, a weak vessel,
an irregular oval,
sat melancholic
in the Udel'naia station.

I had nowhere to hide
the troubles of my soul,
and a petroleum rainbow
blossomed before me.

I'd so worsened and
multiplied my troubles,
I senselessly looked
over the fence across the way.

A psycho-hospital wafted toward me,
its buildings gleaming bright,
and faces quickly glimpsed,
and voices rejoicing,

then they sang whatever came to mind,
switching to a scream,
and from the Finnish swamp
a reed answered them.

В ОТЕЛЕ

Цветной туман, отдельные детали
(как в детстве, прежде чем надел очки;
игра «Летающие колпачки» —
я позабыл, куда они летали).

Конгресс масонов в пестрых колпаках,
крутясь в сигарных облаках слоистых,
сливался с конференцией славистов
и растворялся в нижних кабаках.
Жидомасонский заговор в разгаре:
один масон уже блюет в углу,
слависты пьют, друг другу корчат хари
и лязгают зубами по стеклу.

Случайный славофильный господин,
надравшись в своем номере, один
сидит, жуя тесемки от кальсон,
на краешке кровати пустомерзкой
и ждет, когда с отвесом иль стамеской
ворвется иудей или масон.
Чужбинушка — подмоги ждать откель?
По стенкам бесы корчатся — доколе?

Как колокол, колеблется отель.
Работают лифты на алкоголе.
А это что там, покидая бар,
вдруг загляделось в зеркало, икая,
что за змея жидовская такая?
Ах, это я. Ну, это я ...бал.
От шестисот шестидесяти шести
грамм выпитых, от пошлостей, от дыма
какое там до Иерусалима —
тебе бы до постели доползти.

In the Hotel

A fog of colors, separate details
(as when I was a child, before I wore glasses;
the game of "flying caps"—
I've forgotten where they were flying to).

A congress of Masons in parti-colored caps,
hubbubbing within strata of cigar smoke,
merged with the conference of Slavists
and dissolved in the bar downstairs.
It's a Yid-Masonic conspiracy in full swing:
one Mason is already puking in the corner,
the Slavists are drinking, making faces at each other,
their teeth chattering against their glasses.

An occasional gentleman-Slavophile,
who got plastered in his room,
sits alone, chewing the drawstring of his shorts,
on the edge of his abominably desolate bed,
and waits until a Jew or Mason
breaks in with a plummet or a chisel.
In a foreign land, whence can one expect help?
Demons are twitching on the walls, for how long?

Like a bell, the hotel sways to and fro.
The elevators are running on alcohol.
But what's that there, leaving the bar,
eyes suddenly fixed on the mirror and hiccupping,
what kind of Yid snake is that?
Ah, well, it's me. Well, I'll be .ucked.
From the six hundred and sixty-six grams
I've drunk, from the kitsch, from the smoke,
forget all about Jerusalem—
you better just make it to bed.

ОТКРЫТКА ИЗ НОВОЙ АНГЛИИ. 2

Казису Сая

Древо и Бог. Далеко ль до греха?
Птичьего гама висят вороха.

Свиста и шороха грузный заряд
в животрепещущих кленах,
ошеломленные клены горят,
сломлены в полупоклонах.

Вот чем кончается пенье без слов
веток, полуночный свист их,
листьев касанья, раздвижка стволов
столь тонкогубо дуплистых.

Было о чем нам краснеть в октябре.
Будет вперед нам наука.
Сладко ли корчиться грубой коре
в схватке рождения звука?

Мало ли было подобных наук?
Листья — на землю, а птицы — на юг.

Листья вмерзают в предутренний лед
бурыми сотнями сотен.
Как он бесплотен был, этот налет,
Господи, как мимолетен!

Кончились — птицы, листва и тепло.
Падает снег и чернеет дупло.

Postcard from New England. 2

for Kazys Saja

A tree and God. Can sin be far away?
In the air, heaps of feathered uproar.

An unwieldy charge of singing and rustling
in the palpitating maple trees,
the stunned maples glitter,
bent and arched over.

That's how the wordless song
of the branches ends, their midnight piping,
the rustling of the leaves, the swaying trunks
with their thin-lipped hollows.

There was something for us to blush about in October.
That will be a lesson for us.
Should the coarse bark sweetly convulse
in the throes of the birth of a sound?

Were there few such lessons?
Leaves fall to the ground, and birds fly to the south.

In auburn hundreds of hundreds
the leaves freeze onto the early morning ice.
How insubstantial it was, this deposit,
My Lord, how fleeting!

It's finished: the birds, the leaves, the warmth.
Snow is falling and the hollow in the tree darkens.

СОН

горе подателю сего
он потерял свой паспорт
а гр
растопчина пригласила нас на топталище
будет адмирал шишков
писатели пушков и пешкин
лифшиц тоже обещал заглянуть
а без паспорта не пустят
паралич слов
ильич красок
а в семь часов америка закрывается
и уже поздно

Dream

woe betide the bearer of this
he lost his passport
and mrs.
kindling invited us to a grape-crushing
admiral bigwig will be there
the writers fluffer and pawnish
lifshits also promised to look in
but without a passport he won't get through
palsy de words
ilich de colors
and at seven o'clock america closes
and it's already late

ОТКРЫТКА ИЗ НОВОЙ АНГЛИИ. 3

Отцу

Все птицы улетели, но одна
все мечется, когда перевожу
прощальный взгляд, октябрь благодаря
за то, что взвито все и завито,
бродя в лесу и натыкаясь на
шлагбаум, перекрывающий межу,
кленовый сук, упершийся в ничто,
как робкий посошок поводыря.

В моих глазах есть щелка темноты.
Но зренью моему не овдоветь.
Ведь лучшая для жизни половина
сквозь эту щель все явственней видна.
Прими мой стих, как подаянье, ты,
беспечная богатая страна.
Я в дом впускаю осень Халлоуина,
детишек в виде тыкв и в виде ведьм.

Postcard from New England. 3

for my father

All the birds have left, but one
still rushes about, as I cast
my farewell glance, thanking October,
that everything is wound up and tied up,
wandering in the woods I stumble
across a barrier marking the lot boundary,
a maple bough, propped against nothing,
like a ranger's modest walking stick.

There is a chink of darkness in my eyes.
But my sight will not widow me.
You see, life's better half is all the more
clearly visible through this slit.
Accept my verse as alms,
you rich and carefree land.
At my door I receive Halloween's autumn,
children appearing as pumpkins and witches.

* * *

Я сна не торопил, он сразу состоялся,
и стали сниться сны, тасуясь так и сяк,
и мир из этих снов прекрасный составлялся,
и в этом мире снов я шлялся, как дурак.

Я мертвым говорил взволнованные речи,
я тех, кого здесь нет, хватал за рукава,
и пафос алкаша с настырностью предтечи
буровились во мне, и я качал права.

И отменил я «нет», и упразднил «далече»,
и сам себя до слез растрогал, как в кино.
С отвагой алкаша, с усилием предтечи
проснулся. Серый свет дневной глядит в окно.

Я серый свет дневной. Гляжу в окно: герани,
два хилых стула, сны — второй и третий сорт,
подобие стола (из канцелярской дряни),
на коем вижу не-гативный натюрморт:

недопитый стакан, невыключенная лампа,
счет неоплаченный за телефон и не-
надписанный конверт без марки и без штампа.
Фон: некий человек ничком на простыне.

* * *

I did not hasten sleep, it happened at once,
and the dreams began, shuffling themselves this way and that,
and out of these dreams a wonderful world came into being,
and I loafed around in this dream world like an idiot.

I spoke excitedly to the dead and clutched at
the sleeves of those no longer here,
and the pathos of a drunk with the insolence of a baptist
stormed up in me, and I stood up for my rights.

And I revoked "no" and abolished "far away,"
and moved myself to tears, as in the movies.
With the courage of a drunk and the effort of a baptist
I woke up. The day's grey light peers in at the window.

I am the day's grey light. I peer into the window:
geraniums, two rickety chairs, dreams—second and third rate,
something resembling a desk (made out of office rubbish),
on which I see a ne-gative still life:

a glass not emptied, a lamp not turned off,
a telephone bill not paid, and
an envelope not addressed, without stamp or postmark.
The foreground: a certain person lying prone on a sheet.

МЕСТОИМЕНИЯ

Предательство, которое в крови.
Предать себя, предать свой глаз и палец,
предательство распутников и пьяниц,
но от иного, Боже, сохрани.

Вот мы лежим. Нам плохо. Мы больной.
Душа живет под форточкой отдельно.
Под нами не обычная постель, но
тюфяк-тухляк, больничный перегной.

Чем я, больной, так неприятен мне,
так это тем, что он такой неряха:
на морде пятна супа, пятна страха
и пятна черт чего на простыне.

Еще толчками что-то в нас течет,
когда лежим с озябшими ногами,
и все, что мы за жизнь свою налгали,
теперь нам предъявляет длинный счет.

Но странно и свободно ты живешь
под форточкой, где ветка, снег и птица,
следя, как умирает эта ложь,
как больно ей и как она боится.

Pronouns

The betrayal which is in the blood.
To betray oneself, betray one's eye and finger.
The betrayal of libertines and drunks,
but from *this one*, Lord, preserve us.

Here we are in bed. We're not feeling well. We're a patient.
My soul lives by itself, under the open window vent.
There's not a normal bed beneath us,
but a rotten-cotton mattress, hospital humus.

The reason that I, the sick one, am so
unpleasant to me is that he's such a slob:
soup stains on his ugly mug, stains of fear
and the devil knows what else on his sheets.

Something still flows within us in jolts,
while we lie there with frozen legs,
and every lie we'd uttered our life long
now presents us with a detailed bill.

But you live strangely and freely
under the window vent, among twig, snow and bird,
and watch closely as this lie dies,
following its pain and its fear.

УРОК ФОТОГРАФИИ. 2

В чем дело тут — давайте разберем.
Не в том, что бренны серебро и бром.
Не в выцветшем лице интеллигентном.
А в том, что время светит фонарем.
Или рентгеном.

Смотри — под арматурною стеной
сидит во мне товарищ костяной
и важно отвечает на вопросы
стеклянной водки, кильки жестяной,
бумажной папиросы.

Photography Lesson. 2

What's the point here: let's take a closer look.
It's not that silver and bromide are transitory.
It's not in the faded face of an intellectual.
But rather that time shines like a lantern.
Or like an X-ray.

Look: near the steel-reinforced wall
a skeletal comrade sits within me,
and earnestly answers the questions
posed by some glassy vodka, a tinny sprat,
and a paper cigarette.

* * *

> Роскошный круиз за баснословно
> дешевую цену. Маршрут: Мюнхен —
> Ялта — Хельсинки.
> *Из газет*

Дом
наполнен теплом.
За стеклом
непогода.
Я не знаю, куда мы плывем,
но я чувствую дрожь парохода.
Это, наверное, тысяча восемьсот
год
какой-то из семидесятых.
Мы не знаем, куда нас несет,
пассажиров усатых,
при жилетах, цепочках, хороших манерах, при позитивных началах…
Снег крупой.
Дождь рябой.
Многотонный прибой
молотобой-
ствует в скалах.
Но еще можно кофе сварить,
отворить
толстый томик российских стихов —
«Пир во время чумы»: есть упоение…
Накрахмаленный captain, возглавляющий наш table d'hôte,
нам рассказывает анекдот
(он давно потерял управление
кораблем, но еще зеркала
рассмеются любезно
и еще в четырех миллиметрах стекла
мрак и бездна).

* * *

> *An elegant cruise for a fabulously low price.*
> *The itinerary: Munich - Yalta - Helsinki.*
> From the newspapers

The house
is filled with warmth.
Outside the window
poor weather.
I don't know where we're sailing
but I feel the steamship's shudders.
It's probably eighteen-hundred
and some year
in the seventies.
We don't know where we're being taken,
mustachioed passengers
in waistcoats, watch chains, well-mannered,
                 with auspicious beginnings. . .
Sleet and hail.
Speckled rain.
The multitonned surf
hammers
into the cliffs.
But one can still make coffee,
open
a fat volume of Russian verse—
"A Feast in Time of Plague": there is rapture . . .
The starched captain, at the head of our table d'hôte,
tells us an anecdote
(he lost control of the ship
long ago, but the mirrors still
obligingly burst into laughter,
and the gloom and the abyss are
still separated by four millimeters of glass).

* * *

Что день — то повышается накал
смущения, смятения, тревоги.
Вот нынче утром зайчик прискакал
и, серенький, уселся на пороге.

Он всматривался в глубину жилья
не косо, а скорее косоглазо,
и наползала, сердце тяжеля,
какая-то неясная зараза.

Куда другой его уставлен глаз?
Какие там опасности и беды?
Какие козни поджидают нас —
враги? врачи? литературоведы?

Какие мне замаливать грехи?
Кому писать? Откуда ждать ответа?
Я что-то расписался, а стихи —
вот самая недобрая примета.

* * *

Every day the intensity of confusion,
perplexity and alarm increases.
Just this morning a rabbit hopped up,
dull grey, and settled down on the doorstep.

He peered into the depths of our abode,
looking not askance, but rather cross-eyed,
and some kind of obscure contagion,
making the heart grow heavy, crawled in.

Where was his other eye focused?
What kind of dangers and disasters are there?
What intrigues lie in wait for us:
enemies? doctors? literary scholars?

For what sins must I atone?
To whom should I write? Whence await a reply?
I've somehow written too much, and verses—
they're the worst of omens.

ОДИН ДЕНЬ ЛЬВА ВЛАДИМИРОВИЧА

Перемещен из Северной и Новой
Пальмиры и Голландии, живу
здесь нелюдимо в Северной и Новой
Америке и Англии. Жую
из тостера изъятый хлеб изгнанья
и ежеутренне взбираюсь по крутым
ступеням белокаменного зданья,
где пробавляюсь языком родным.
Развешиваю уши. Каждый звук
калечит мой язык или позорит.

Когда состарюсь, я на старый юг
уеду, если пенсия позволит.
У моря над тарелкой макарон
дней скоротать остаток по-латински,
слезою увлажняя окоем,
как Бродский, как, скорее, Баратынский.
Когда последний покидал Марсель,
как пар пыхтел и как пилась марсала,
как провожала пылкая мамзель,
как мысль плясала, как перо писало,
как в стих вливался моря мерный шум,
как в нем синела дальняя дорога,
как не входило в восхищенный ум,
как оставалось жить уже немного.

One Day in the Life of Lev Vladimirovich

Displaced from the Northern and New
Palmyra and Holland, I lead a
reclusive life in the Northern and New
America and England. I chew the bread
of exile confiscated from the toaster and
each morning clamber up the steep
steps of the white stone building,
where I get by on my native tongue.
I listen on open-mouthed. Each sound
maims or disgraces my language.

When I grow old, I'll head for
the old south, if my pension permits.
I'll while away the remainder of my days
in the Latin style, by the sea over
a plate of pasta, moistening my horizon
with a tear, like Brodsky or rather Baratynsky.
When the latter was leaving Marseilles,
how the steam puffed and the Marsala was quaffed,
how that ardent mamselle accompanied him,
how his thoughts danced, how his pen wrote,
how the measured surge of the sea flowed into his verse,
how the distant road gleamed cerulean in it,
how the enraptured senses were spared the thought,
how little time he had left to live.

Однако что зевать по сторонам.
Передо мною сочинений горка.
«Тургенев любит написать роман
Отцы с Ребенками». Отлично, Джо, пятерка!
Тургенев любит поглядеть в окно.
Увидеть нив зеленое рядно.
Рысистый бег лошадки тонконогой.
Горячей пыли пленку над дорогой.
Ездок устал, в кабак он завернет.
Не евши, опрокинет там косушку...
И я в окно — а за окном Вермонт,
соседний штат, закрытый на ремонт,
на долгую весеннюю просушку.
Среди покрытых влагою холмов
каких не понапрятано домов,
какую не увидишь там обитель:
в одной укрылся нелюдимый дед,
он в бороду толстовскую одет
и в сталинский полувоенный китель.
В другой живет поближе к небесам
кто, словеса плетя витиевато,
с глубоким пониманьем описал
лирическую жизнь дегенерата.

Задавши студиозусам урок,
берем газету (глупая привычка).
Ага, стишки. Конечно, «уголок»,
«колонка» или, сю-сю-сю, «страничка».
По Сеньке шапка. Сенькин перепрыг
из комсомольцев прямо в богомольцы
свершен. Чем нынче потчуют нас в рыг-
-аловке? Угодно ль гонобольцы?
Все постненькое, Божии рабы?
Дурные рифмы. Краденые шутки.
Накушались. Спасибо. Как бобы
шевелятся холодные в желудке.

But enough gawking about.
Before me lies a mountain of papers.
"Turgenev loves to have written the novel
Fathers and Childs." Excellent, Joe, an A!
Turgenev loves to look out the window.
To watch the green sackcloth of the cornfields.
The trot of a slim-legged horse.
The film of hot dust above the road.
The rider is tired, he'll stop by an inn.
Without eating, he'll knock back half a liter . . .
I too look out the window, and past the window lies Vermont,
my neighboring state, closed for repairs,
for its long springtime drying-out.
Among the hills swathed in mist,
you wouldn't believe the houses tucked away,
every kind of abode you could imagine.
In one a grandpa recluse has hidden himself,
dressed in a Tolstoyan beard
and a Stalinist paramilitary jacket.
In another, living closer to heaven,
lives he who, weaving words ornately,
described with profound understanding
the lyrical life of a degenerate.

With the lesson delivered to the sciolists,
we take up a newspaper (a stupid habit).
Uh-oh, some verses. Naturally, a "nook,"
"column," or, tsk, tsk, tsk, "little page."
He got his just deserts, he just deserted
right from the Komsomols intact into God's devout.
What do they regale us with today in belch—
fishing? Would you like some bilberries?
Everything nicely lenten, servants of God?
Stupid rhymes. Stolen jokes.
We've had our fill. Thank you.
Like cold beans stirring in the stomach.

Смеркается. Пора домой. Журнал
московский, что ли, взять как веронал.
Там олух размечтался о былом,
когда ходили наши напролом
и сокрушали нечисть помелом,
а эмигранта отдаленный предок
деревню одарял полуведром.
Крути, как хочешь, русский палиндром
барин и раб, читай хоть так, хоть эдак,
не может раб существовать без бар.
Сегодня стороной обходим бар.

Там хорошо. Там стелется, слоист,
сигарный дым. Но там сидит славист.
Опасно. До того опять допьюсь,
что перед ним начну метать свой бисер
и от коллеги я опять добьюсь,
чтоб он опять в ответ мне пошлость высер:
«Ирония не нужно казаку,
you sure could use some domestication, *
недаром в вашем русском языку
такого слова нет — sophistication». **

Есть слово «истина». Есть слово «воля».
Есть из трех букв — «уют». И «хамство» есть.
Как хорошо в ночи без алкоголя
слова, что невозможно перевести,
бредя, пространству бормотать пустому.
На слове «падло» мы подходим к дому.

* "you sure could use some domestication" — "уж вам бы пошло на пользу малость дрессировки."
** sophistication — очень приблизительно: "изысканность."

It's getting dark. Time to go home. Why not
take the Moscow journal along as barbital.
An idiot in it was raving about the past,
when our fellows forged ahead,
and wiped out the scum clean away,
but a distant forefather of an émigré
gave his village half a bucket.
Twist the Russian palindrome "*barin i rab*"
anyway you wish, read it this way or that,
a servant cannot exist without the gentry.
Today we'll give the bar a wide berth.

It's good there. The cigar smoke slowly
spreads in a layer. But a Slavist is sitting there.
Danger. Will I drink so much again that
I'll start to cast my pearls before him,
and once again drive my colleague
to shit out a vulgar banality once again in reply:
"A Cossack don't need irony,
you sure could use some domestication,
there's a reason that your Russianese
language has no word for 'sophistication'."

There is the word "truth." And the word "will."
And the seven-lettered "comfort." And there's "boorishness."
How nice it is, ambling at night without alcohol,
to murmur to the empty reaches
words impossible to translate.
We arrive home on the word "shithead."

Дверь за собой плотней прикрыть, дабы
в дом не прокрались духи перекрестков.
В разношенные шлепанцы стопы
вставляй, поэт, пять скрюченных отростков.
Еще проверь цепочку на двери.
Приветом обменяйся с Пенелопой.
Вздохни. В глубины логова прошлепай.
И свет включи. И вздрогни. И замри:
... А это что еще такое?

А это — зеркало, такое стеклецо,
чтоб увидать со щеткой за щекою
судьбы перемещенное лицо.

Close the door tight behind you,
lest the spirits of the crossroads steal into the house.
Place into your well-worn slippers, poet,
the five writhing sprouts of your foot.
Check the chain on the door once more.
Exchange greetings with Penelope.
Sigh. Shuffle off into the depths of your lair.
Turn on the light. And shudder. And freeze:
. . . And what is that?

That's a mirror, just a piece of glass,
so that you can see, with the brush inside your mouth,
the displaced face of fate.

НОРКОВЫЙ РУЧЕЙ

Подражание Фросту

– Где север, Леша?

– Север, Нина, там,
поскольку наш ручей течет на запад.

День был проглочен с горем пополам,
не позолочен и ничем не запит,
и то, что в горле вечером торчит,
горчит, как будто ты три дня не емши.
Восходят звезды и ручей ворчит.

– Вообще, согласно Фросту, штат Нью-Хэмпшир
тем характерен, что его ручьи,
как правило, направлены к востоку.

– Так что, ручей, ворчи там не ворчи,
но ты бежишь неправильно, без толку.

– Оставь его, пускай живет один.

– А может, он повернут был, но кем же?

– Да нет, он, слава Богу, без плотин.
Вообще, согласно Фросту, штат Нью-Хэмпшир
нас от большого бизнеса хранит,
нас от избытка охраняет зорко.
Единственное разве что гранит
для мертвецов Бостона и Нью-Йорка —
вот все, что мы имеем поставлять.

Mink Brook

        (after Robert Frost)

—Where's north, Lyosha?

                —North's is that way, Nina,
since our brook flows west.

The day was just barely swallowed, a grievous feat,
like an unsweetened pill with nothing to wash it down,
and what sticks in the throat tonight
tastes bitter, as if you hadn't eaten for three days.
The stars are rising and the brook is grumbling.

—In general, according to Frost, the state
of New Hampshire is distinctive in that its brooks,
as a rule, flow towards the east.

—Therefore, brook, you may grumble all you want,
but you're running in the wrong direction, senselessly.

—Lay off it, let it live alone.

—Or perhaps it was turned, but, by whom?

—No thank God, it hasn't a dam.
In general, according to Frost, the state
of New Hampshire preserves us from big business,
vigilantly protecting us from plenty.
And really the one and only thing
that we can produce is granite
for the deceased in Boston and New York.

А впрочем есть вода, довольно леса,
но все же не довольно, чтоб сплавлять,
что, стало быть, не может представлять
коммерческого интереса.
Но на зиму здесь всем хватает дров,
и яблок впрок для пирогов и сидра,
на шапки местным жителям бобров
хватает, а порой блеснет и выдра.
Опять же лес дает нам лес на кров
(опять же не в количестве товарном),
и молока от собственных коров
вполне хватает нашим сыроварням.
И если расстараться, наконец,
то можно золотишка в этих реках
намыть за год на парочку колец,
конечно, тонких, но отменно крепких.

— Фрост Красный Нос.

                        — Нет, нос был желтоват.
И весь он был — не желтизною воска,
а как желтеют яблоки, как сад
под осень, как закатная полоска,
как лампочка в свои под сотню ватт,
как, прежде чем погаснуть, папироска,
как пальцы у курильщика желтят.

— О'кей, о'кей. Изменим наш куплет.
Фрост Желтый Нос. Или какой был нос-то?

— На родине я прожил сорок лет
без малого.

        — А он?

But then again there is water, and enough wood,
but all the same not enough to float downstream
and consequently, is unable
to attract commercial interest.
But there's enough firewood for everyone
to lay up for winter, and plenty of apples for pies and cider,
and enough beavers to crown the heads of the locals,
now and then even a glossy otter rides by.
Once again the forests give us wood for shelter
(once again not in marketable quantity),
and the milk from our own cows
quite suffices for our cheesemakers.
And, if you truly set yourself to it, then you
could pan enough gold in a year's time
out of these rivers to make a couple of rings,
thin ones of course, but extraordinarily strong.

—Frost the Red-Nosed.

                    —No, his nose was yellowish.
As was all of him—not the sallow hue of candle wax,
but rather as apples yellow, like an orchard
towards autumn, like a swath of sunset,
like a light bulb of meager wattage,
like a cigarette just before it goes out,
or the way a smoker's fingers yellow.

—Okay, okay. Let's change our stanza.
Frost the Yellow-Nosed. Or how was the nose?

—I lived almost forty years in my
homeland.

        —And he?

– Он девяносто.
И, все же, эмигрировал, как мы,
туда, где свет имеет форму тьмы,
где тьма есть звук, где звук звучит, как вата,
туда, где нет ни лета, ни зимы…

– «Туда, туда, откуда нет возврата!»

– Да как сказать. А наших кто речей
сейчас предмет, их тема, их значенье?
Кто нам опять кивает на ручей
и просит рассмотреть его теченье?
Там вечно возвращается вода —
удар о камень и бросок обратно.
Пусть это мимолетно, но всегда…

– Пусть пустячок, а все-таки приятно!
А ежели серьезно, книгочей,
то это — «дань течения истоку».

Так мимо наших дней, трудов, ночей
течет на запад Норковый ручей.
Все прочие ручьи текут к востоку.

              —Ninety years.
And all the same he emigrated, like we did,
to that land where the light has the contours of darkness,
where darkness is a sound, where the sound sounds, like cotton,
where there is no summer, no winter . . .

—"There, whence no one returns!"

—Yes, you could put it that way. But whom are
we talking about now, what subject, what meaning?
Who nods once again to the brook
and asks us to ponder its current?
There the water eternally returns:
its dash against the stone and its recoil backwards.
And though it be momentary, it is always so . . .

—Even if it's a trifle, it's pleasing all the same!
But if taken seriously, bibliophile,
then this is "the current's tribute to its source."

Thus does Mink Brook flow towards the west,
past our days, our works, our nights.
All the other brooks flow towards the east.

МОЯ КНИГА

Ни Риму, ни миру, ни веку,
ни в полный внимания зал —
в Летейскую библиотеку,
как злобно Набоков сказал.

В студеную зимнюю пору
(«однажды» — за гранью строки)
гляжу, поднимается в гору
(спускается к брегу реки)

усталая жизнь телега,
наполненный хворостью воз.
Летейская библиотека,
готовься к приему всерьез.

Я долго надсаживал глотку
и вот мне награда за труд:
не бросят в Харонову лодку,
на книжную полку воткнут.

My Book

Not to Rome, not to the world, not to the epoch,
not into a full and hushed lecture hall,
but to the "Lethean Library,"
as Nabokov spitefully said.

In the icy season of winter
("one day" overreached the line),
I watch it climbing up the hill
(it will drop down to the river),

the weary coach of life,
a wagon full of disease.
O Lethean Library,
prepare to receive it solemnly.

I strained my gullet a long time,
and this is the reward of my labors:
they won't toss me into Charon's bark,
but will stick me on a bookshelf.

Из книги *Тайный советник*

From *Privy Councilor*

«ЛЕБЕДЬ ПОТА ШИПА РАН»

> Многоступенчатая нордическая метафора
> (кеннинг): *шип ран — меч: пот меча — кровь: лебедь
> крови — ворон.*

1

В доме варежки вяжут варяжки,
в доме тихо, тепло, полумрак.
В генеральской тужурке, фуражке
на войну уезжает варяг.

В генеральской тужурке и стрижке
волосок к волоску, полубокс,
и, полвека привычно остривший,
произносит швейцар: «Полубог-с».

Сквозь зеркальные стекла подъезда
Дочь-курсистка угрюмо глядит.
Черный паккард срывается с места.
Черный ворон на битву летит.

2

Для филолога это не диво,
карандашик слегка обведет,
и липковатом комке генитива
предсказуемы «меч», «кровь» и «пот».

Чу, часы заворочались — девять.
Библиограф подходит опять.
Остается невыяснен «лебедь».
На столе позабыта тетрадь.

Невский умер. Подходит девятка
и увозит в туман, гололедь.
Ах, надолго забыта тетрадка!
Белый лебедь остался белеть.

"The Swan of the Sweat of the Thorn of Wounds"

> a multi-tiered Nordic metaphor (kenning):
> "thorn of wounds" = "sword"; "sweat of the sword" = "blood";
> "swan of blood" = "raven"

1

In the house the Varangian women are knitting mittens,
in the house it is quiet, warm, penumbral.
In a general's double-breasted jacket and peak-cap
the Varangian rides off to war.

In a general's jacket and haircut,
each hair aligned, a semibutch cut,
with his casual, half-century old wit,
the doorman said, "You're a demigod."

The student-daughter looks morosely
through the plateglass windows of the vestibule.
The black Packard tears off.
The black raven flies to battle.

2

For the philologist it's nothing extraordinary,
he draws the pencil lightly along,
and in the sticky lump of a genitive
"sword", "blood," and "sweat" are foretold.

Hark, the clock has begun to turn 9.
The bibliographer is coming by again.
"Swan" remains unexplicated.
On the table a notebook lies forgotten.

Nevsky's dead. The number 9 arrives
and bears me off into the fog and icy roads.
Ah, the notebook will be lost for a long time!
The white swan remained behind to whiten.

3

Пациенты боятся наркоза,
но сдаются в тоске и слезах.
Рваной раны огромная роза
распускалась у всех на глазах.

Ковыряясь в глубинах разреза,
уже просто рукой без ножа
извлекая из мяса железо,
пел: «Пощади никто не жела...»

Медсестра с драгоценною ватой
подошла ему лоб обтереть,
и мгновенно комок сероватый
кровь и пот пропитали на треть.

4

«Слово о половецком разгроме,
о «Варяге», идущем ко дну,
Ермаке перед смертью в истоме —
все сливается в тему одну».

Подготовлен доклад к семинару.
Вдруг, при поиске беглом ключей,
хмурый взгляд упирается в пару
на тужурке скрещенных мечей.

На мгновенье отбросило фото
для фотографа сделанный вид?
Или стукнула дверь? Иль всего-то
запах шипра? Но меч глянцевит.

* * *

Запах шипра, но меч, глянцевит,
кровь и пот пропитали на треть.
Черный ворон на битву летит.
Белый лебедь остался белеть.

3

The patients fear the anesthesia,
but they surrender in tears and anguish.
The great rose of the ripped wound
blossomed in everyone's eyes.

Groping about in the depths of the slit,
just using his hand, without a knife,
then extracting metal from the flesh,
he was singing, "And no one sought mercy . . ."

A nurse approached to wipe
his brow with priceless cotton,
and at once a third of the grayish wad
was suffused with blood and sweat.

4

"The Lay of the Polovtsian defeat,
of the 'Varangian' going under,
of Yermak's languid ease before death,
it all merges into one theme."

With the report for the seminar finished,
while he hurriedly searches for his keys,
suddenly his sullen glance falls upon
a pair of crossed swords on a double-breasted jacket.

Did the photo momentarily hurl back
the pose struck for the photographer?
Or was there a knock at the door? Or is it all
only the odor of cologne? But the sword gleams.

* * *

The odor of cologne, but the sword, gleaming,
a third suffused with blood and sweat.
The black raven flies to battle.
The white swan remained behind to whiten.

3 РУБЛЯ

Случай в Москве

В котельной
багров кагор близ колбасы отдельной.

И вдруг на трех рублях, где будто б злак,
он распознал масонский знак,
а в самой цифре 3
узрел звезду Давида.
Похолодело все внутри,
но он не подал вида.

Гремело радио, бодря,
всех призывая на заря-
дку. Встала над Москвой заря
тридцать второго мартобря.

Он принял в сквере двести грамм
и наблюдал, дремля,
свеченье красных пентаграмм
над башнями Кремля.
Он спал, но то был вещий сон,
в нем было 5 идей:
1) имеют башни облик свеч;
2) их ясно кто сумел возжечь;
3) Фиораванти — иудей;
4) Наполеон — масон;
5) . . . .

3 Rubles
(an occurrence in Moscow)

In the boiler house the port wine
appears crimson beside the cheap sausage.

And suddenly on a 3-rouble note, as if it were a stalk of grain,
he recognized a Masonic sign,
and in the very number 3
he espied the star of David.
Everything went cold inside him,
but he didn't show it.

The radio thundered with gusto,
exhorting all to their gymnastic
exercises. The sun rose above Moscow
on the thirty-second of Marchember.

In the park he drank back two hundred grams
and drowsily observed
the red pentagrams shining
above the Kremlin towers.
He slept, but it was a prophetic sleep,
with 5 ideas during it:
1) the towers have the appearance of candles;
2) it's clear who was able to light them;
3) Fioravanti was a Jew;
4) Napoleon was a Mason;
5) . . . .

Оплывал потихоньку красный воск,
и левый мозг за правый мозг
поехал кое-как.
К себе домой через Крымский мост
шагает кочегар.
Из чувств он ощущал — тоску.
Он понимал, что проиграл
тому, кто хозяйничал в мозгу
и бодро ручки потирал,
и инструменты выбирал.
«Идем к тебе». «Идем ко мне».

Жена на службе. Суп на окне.
Ребенком воздух весь пропах.
Диавол был во всех углах.

Проснулся он от тишины.
Все еще не было жены.
Он чувствовал конец игры.
Он знал, чтó было тишиной,
но брел проверить — не мокры
пеленки дочери грудной?
О да, мокры они, мокры.

The red wax was softly guttering,
the left side of the brain
somehow fell behind the right.
The stoker marches homeward
across the Krymsky bridge.
Of the emotions he felt longing.
He realized that he had lost to
the one who keeps house in his brain,
who blithely rubs his hands together,
as he selects his instruments.
"Let's go to your place." "Let's go to my place."

The wife is at work. Soup's waiting on the sill.
The air saturated with the smell of an infant.
The devil was in every corner.

He awoke because of the stillness.
His wife was still not there.
He sensed the game was up.
He knew *what* that silence was,
but walked around to make sure:
is his infant daughter's diaper wet?
Oh yes, it's wet, it's wet.

DE PROFUNDIS

Лежит на стойке друг-котище,
глазища зеленей со сна.
Я говорю: «Налей, трактирщик,
зеленого налей вина,
налей мне чарку зелена».

Трактирщик говорит: «Ну, Леш,
ну, что ты, Леша, воду мутишь?
Я бы налил, да как нальешь!
Ну, а налью — как пить-то будешь?
Иди, иди, и так хорош».

Я бы пошел, да как пойдешь —
не вытянуть подошв из ила.
«Извозчик, друг, не подвезешь?»
«Один подвез … Куда — чудило!»
Зеленый плещется овес.

А эта церковь как была,
да только поп уплыл куда-то,
и бирюзовы купола,
а золото зеленовато.
А вот и рыбка подплыла.

Улыбкой рыбкин рот распорот.
Вот в китель влит порядка страж.
Уж он-то, знать, залил за ворот.
Так возвращаюсь я в наш город.
Ах, рыбка, рыбка, что мне дашь?

De Profundis

My feline friend lies on the bar,
his eyes more green from sleep.
I say: "Taverner, pour me,
pour me some green wine,
pour me a tankard of the green stuff."

The taverner says: "Now Lyosh,
why do you want to muddy the waters?
I'd pour you some, and how'd I pour!
But, if I serve you, how will you drink it?
Go on now. It's better if you go."

I'd leave, and how'd I leave,
but I can't pull my feet out of the silt.
"Cabby, friend, can you give me a lift?"
"I once gave one a lift to . . . it was bizarre!"
The green oats are splashing.

This church is just as it was,
only the priest disappeared
and the cupolas are turquoise,
and the gold is greenish.
Just then a fish swam up.

The piscine mouth is unstitched by a smile.
The custodian of public order is poured into his uniform.
It looks as though he's already drunk to the gills.
Thus I return to our city.
Ah fish, fish, what will you give me?

* * *

Поэт есть перегной, в нем мертвые слова
сочатся, лопаясь, то щелочно, то кисло,
звук избавляется от смысла, а
аз, буки и т. д. обнажены, как числа,

улыбка тленная уста его свела,
и мысль последняя, как корешок, повисла.
Потом личинка лярвочку прогрызла,
бактерия дите произвела.

Поэт есть перегной.
В нем все пути зерна,
то дождик мочит их, то солнце прогревает.

Потом идет зима,
и белой пеленой
пустое поле покрывает.

* * *

A poet is compost, in him dead words
ooze out, bursting apart, sometimes alkaline, sometimes acidic,
Sound escapes from sense, and
the ABCs, letters, etc. are uncovered, like numbers,

a smile, prone to decay, united his lips,
and his final thought, like a rootlet, was left hanging.
Then a maggot consumed the little *larva*,
bacterium produced children.

A poet is compost.
In him lie all paths of grain,
moistened by showers, warmed by the sun.

Then winter comes,
and covers the empty field
with a white shroud.

В ГРОССБУХ

Я по природе из тетерь.
Не перечесть моих потерь —
стихов, приятелей, ключей,
в дымину пропитых ночей;
то телефонный разговор
похитит полчаса, как вор,
то дети как-то без затей
вдруг выросли — и нет детей.
Я давеча, страшась сумы,
у дара своего взаймы
решил спросить. Какой удар!
Мне отказал мой дивный дар.
И ты, Брут! Так сказать, et tu!
И ты показываешь тыл?
А Муза Памяти? Тю-тю,
ее давно и след простыл.
А Муза Разума? Она
сама в себе отражена
и не дает, зараза, в долг.
Мой лучший друг, Тамбовский Волк,
мотает серой головой:
я, дескать, сам пустой, хоть вой.
Давно уж Музы ни гу-гу,
давно уже сидит в мозгу
бухгалтер, а точней — чекист.
Командует взять чистый лист,
число поставить, месяц, год
и записать: в расход.

In the Ledger

By nature I'm a dunderhead.
There's no tallying up my losses—
verses, friends, keys,
drunken nights lost in a smoky haze;
here, a telephone conversation
will steal a half hour, like a thief,
there, children somehow simply
grow up suddenly—and disappear.
And recently, fearing beggary,
I decided to ask my talent
for a loan. What a blow!
My wondrous gift refused me.
And you, Brutus! That is, et tu!
You're turning your back to me?
And the Muse of Memory? Vanished,
even her track went cold long ago.
And the Muse of Reason? She's
reflected into herself, and
the scourge, she doesn't give credit.
My best friend, Tambovsky Wolf,
shakes his grey head: claims that
he's empty himself, you could just howl.
For ages, not a peep from the Muses,
For ages in my brain sits
a bookkeeper, or rather, a Chekist.
He orders: take a clean sheet,
record the day, month, year
and make a note—to write off.

ЛЕВЛОСЕВ

Левлосев не поэт, не кифаред.
Он маринист, он велимировед,
бродскист в очках и с реденькой бородкой,
он осиполог с сиплой глоткой,
он пахнет водкой,
он порет бред.

Левлосевлосевлосевлосевон–
онононононононон иуда,
он предал Русь, он предает Сион,
он пьет лосьон,
не отличает добра от худа,
он никогда не знает, что откуда,
хоть слышал звон.

Он аннофил, он александроман,
федоролюб, переходя на прозу,
его не станет написать роман,
а там статью по важному вопросу —
держи карман!

Он слышит звон,
как будто кто казнен
там, где солома якобы едома,
но то не колокол, то телефон,
он не подходит, его нет дома.

Levlosev

Levlosev is not a poet, not a citharoede.
He's a Marinist, a Velimirician,
a bespectacled Brodskyite with a thinning beard,
he's an Osipologist with a raw esophagus,
he reeks of vodka,
he rants gibberish.

Levlosevlosevlosevlosevhe—
hehehehehehehe is a Judas,
he betrayed Russia, he's betraying Zion,
he drinks aftershave,
can't tell good from evil,
he never knows from whence it comes,
though he's heard the ringing.

He's an Annophile, an Aleksandromaniac,
a Fyodor-fan, when it comes to prose,
he's not up to writing a novel,
but by and by an article on a vital topic—
don't hold your breath!

He hears the tolling,
as if someone were being executed
there, where the thatch is reputedly edible,
but that's no church bell, only the telephone,
and he doesn't pick up, he's not at home.

ДВЕНАДЦАТЪ КОЛЛЕГИЙ.

Элегия в трех частях

*

Бог умер.
   Ницше.
  Ницше умер.
   Бог[1].

В уборной стонет сизый голубок.
За дверью 00 (два нуля) хорал воды проточной,
И посетитель беспорточный
средь мрамора сидит, как полубог.

Усвоив шутку с зеркалом внутри,
неспешным оком осмотри
сырые стены мраморной пещеры.
Здесь части тел ведут свою войну,
забыв предохранительные меры,
ужасные в длину и в ширину.

...бог умер ницше : ницше умер бог...
Напухших пушек дула смотрят вбок
поверх бойниц курчавых. Из бойниц же,
раскрытых между ног, как третий глаз,
на нас глядит не Бог, не Ницше,
незнамо что глядит на нас.

---

[1] Граффити, часто встречающееся на стенах университетских уборных в США.

Twelve Colleges
An Elegy in Three Parts

*

God is dead.
Nietzsche.
Nietzsche is dead.
God.[1]

A blue-grey pigeon groans in the bathroom.
Behind door 00 (two zeroes) there's a chorale of running water
and the trouserless visitor
sits amid the marble like a demigod.

When you've mastered the trick with the mirror inside,
take in with an unhurried eye
the damp walls of the marble cave.
Here the bodies' units, terrible in length and breadth,
having forgotten their protective measures,
wage their own war.

. . . *god is dead nietzsche : nietzsche is dead god* . . .
The barrels of swollen canons peer sideways
atop the curly embrasures, out of which,
opened between the legs, like a third eye,
not God, not Nietzsche gazes at us,
something unknown gazes at us.

---

[1] Graffiti, often seen on the walls of university bathrooms in the USA.

**

Дом, именуемый глаголом — «лгу»,
пустынных волн стоял на берегу
и вдаль глядел. Пред ним неслись «победы»,
троллейбусы, профессоры, народ,
красавицы и наоборот,
и будущие эзоповеды.
За чтенье на картошке «Also sprach…»
ах, некогда мне было там sehr schwach.
Я там узнал, что комсомол неистов,
что что бы я им там не плел, козел,
из этих алкашей и онанистов
со мной никто б в разведку не пошел,
что я — змея, побег дурной травы,
что должен быть растоптан и раздавлен.

Но тут примчался папа из Москвы,
просил, и я был, так и быть, оставлен.

Я на допросе препирался с про–
(зачеркнуто) — на зачете с Проппом.
Я думал сказки — то, се, зло, добро,
а Пропп считал избушку гробом.[1]

---

[1] См. В. Я. Пропп «Исторические корни волшебной сказки».

**

The building named the verb "I lie"
stood on a shore of desolate waves
and gazed into the distance. "Victories," trolleybuses,
professors and crowds rushed past it,
beautiful girls and those that weren't,
and future Aesopians.
Caught in the potato fields reading "Also Sprach . . ."
ach, back then I became kind of *sehr schwach*.
I realized then, that the Komsomol is rabid,
that, no matter what I drivelled, bastard,
not one of those boozers and onanists
would take me on a reconnaissance mission,
that I was a serpent, a wisp of an evil weed
that must be trampled down and stamped out.

But just then Papa came tearing in from Moscow,
made appeals, and, as it goes, I was left alone.

At the hearing I wrangled with the prosec-
(crossed out)—on account of Propp.
I thought fairy tales were this and that, good and evil,
but Propp thought a peasant hut to be a coffin.[1]

---

[1] Cf. V. Ya. Propp "Historical Roots of the Fairytale."

И Пропп был прав, а я не прав. И вот
ко мне избушка повернулась задом.
В разведку не был послан я отрядом,
но поворот мне вышел от ворот,
где забивает целый день козла,
а польт не принимает гардеробщик,
где темная Нева под льдами ропщет
извне добра и зла.

***

Университет похмельной лиги.
На железных полках дрыхнут книги.
Перестрелка теннисных мячей.
Все всегда кончается ничьей.

Старички в штанишках сухопары
и старушки (смешанные пары).
Скованный склероз телодвиже-
ний, как пары рифм: две *м*, две *ж*.

Теннисная схватка без ракетки.
Пишущая машинка без каретки.
Пыльное, без форточки окно.
Темновато. Впрочем, не темно.

Прогуляться возле стадиона.
Не студено? Вроде, не студено.
Но нельзя сказать, чтобы тепло.
Два овала вялых на табло.

And Propp was right, and I was wrong. And then
the hut turned its backside to me.
I wasn't sent on a recon mission by the detachment,
although indeed I got the gate,
where, playing dominoes all day,
the cloakroom attendant won't take my coat,
where the dark Neva murmurs
under the ice, beyond good and evil.

***

A university of the hangover league.
Books snooze on the metal shelves.
Hostile volleys of tennis balls.
Everything always ends in a draw.

"Senior league" men in shorts and old ladies
are skinny (mixed doubles).
The movements of their sclerosis-
bound bodies, like doubled rhymes: two Ms, two Fs.

A tennis rumble without a racket.
A typewriter without a carriage.
A dusty window without a window vent.
It's dusky. But not dark.

Should we take a stroll round the stadium.
Isn't it freezing outside? It's not exactly
freezing, but you can't say it's warm.
Two flabby ovals on the scoreboard.

* * *

Памяти А. А. Тарковского

Стерва ворона закаркала,
не удержалась, трепло.
Публика с берега зыркала.
Нерукотворное зеркало
к нам по реке приплыло.

Вот ведь какое сокровище.
Что же, помолимся, прах,
перед свечой несгорающей,
глядя на строгий стареющий
лик в близоруких очках.

* * *

To the Memory of A. A. Tarkovsky

The raven's corpse began to caw,
couldn't refrain, the chatterbox.
The audience on the riverbank cast glances.
A mirror, not made by human hands,
approached us along the water.

Well, indeed what a treasure.
Alright then, let us pray, ashes,
before an eternal candle,
looking at the severe and aging
face wearing thick eyeglasses.

НЕСОБРАННОЕ

Uncollected

АЛЛЕГОРИЯ

Правильно поют в Артеке дети:
«Коммунизм шагает по планете».

Он шагает грузно и неловко,
вляпывается в кучи и ворчит,
и задорная его боеголовка
из ширинки незастегнутой торчит.

Allegory

What the children sing in Artek is correct:
"Communism is marching across the planet."

It marches heavily and clumsily,
stumbling into everything and growling,
and its quick-tempered warhead
hangs out of its unbuttoned fly.

Lev Loseff, ca. 1980.
Photo by Natasha Sharymova from the Loseff family collection.

NOTES to translations

The Last Romance

sentry's bayonet: continues the epigraph from Feodor Glinka's poem "The Prisoner's Song" ("Песнь узника" 1826), which became a popular romance. The opening lines read:

Не слышно шуму городского,	Unheard is the city's din,
В заневских башнях тишина!	Quiet are the towers across the Neva.
И на штыке у часового	And on the sentry's bayonet
Горит полночная луна!	Gleams the midnight moon!

syringe of the Admirality: original "*Адмиралтейства шприц*" alludes to "needle of the Admirality" ("*Адмиралтейства игла*"), Pushkin's metaphor for the building's spire (Russian "*шпиц*"), in his poem "The Bronze Horseman" ("Медный всадник" 1833).

premature baby: cf. Evgeny Baratynsky's poem "Premature" ("Недоносок" 1835).

The Regiment of Eros

Tinkle on, cymbal!: Cf. 1 Corinthians 13:1.

Conversation with a New York Poet

elephant and pug dog: cf. the fable "Elephant and Pug" ("Слон и моська" 1808) by Ivan Krylov.

Korean airliner: On September 1, 1983, a South Korean 747, flight 007, inadvertently strayed into Soviet airspace and was shot down by a Soviet fighter pilot; all 262 passengers were killed. In his autobiographical sketch "Москвы от Лосеффа" (*Меандр* [Москва: новое издательство, 2010], 364), Loseff writes that this "evil deed of the Soviet Air Force" was the impetus for the creation of the poem.

Grounded by Foul Weather

PTU: Polytechnical University, roughly equivalent to a second-rate technical trade school in the USA.

Herostratus: achieved fame by burning down the temple to Artemis in Ephesos in 356 BCE, according to legend during the night in which Alexander was born.

Belomor: cheap shag-tobacco cigarettes.

M

M: each metro station in Moscow is adorned with a bright red "M" above its entrance.

snigger ("скалозуб"): an inversion of "зубоскал," a "scoffer"; "Скалозуб" is a character's surname in Aleksandr Griboedov's play *Woe From Wit* (*Горе от ума* 1823).

Kalinin: Mikhail Ivanovich Kalinin (1875–1946), Bolshevik revolutionary, nominal leader of the Soviet Union and ally of Joseph Stalin.

Lumumba: at the time this poem was written, Patrice Lumumba University in Moscow educated students from the Third World, many believed in the traditions of the KGB. The university now welcomes Russian students as well and is called "Peoples' Friendship University."

The Petrograd Side

that it seemed to be alive: quotation from Aleksandr Pushkin's historical novel *The Captain's Daughter* (*Капитанская дочка* 1836).

In Memory of Moscow

Diamat, Histmat: Soviet abbreviations for dialectical materialism and historical materialism.

instant liver: paronomastic combination of two scarce delicacies in the Soviet Union, instant coffee and canned cod liver.

cement went to tooth fillings: in his memoirs Loseff recounts that he inverted a story told by an acquaintance of how the most expensive, finest cement for tooth fillings in the USA was bought by the Soviets for building the exclusive apartments in "Tsarkoe Selo" earmarked for high-ranking officials in the Ministry of Foreign Trade. Cf. "Москвы от Лосеффа," *Меандр* (Москва: новое издательство, 2010), 385–387.

Don't Arise…: allusion to the Russian lyrics of the "Internationale" "Вставай проклятьем заклеймённый…"

In Memory of Pskov

Gazik: small truck produced by the Gorky motor works.

where the grass is always greener: original alludes to the winged words "там хорошо, где нас нет" ("things are better wherever we're not"), originally from Aleksandr Griboedov's play *Woe From Wit* (*Горе от ума* 1823).

mushrooms with eyes: alludes to the saying "And we in Ryazan have mushrooms with eyes; they are eaten, but they watch," the meaning of which remains obscure.

Fet: Afanasy A. Fet (1820–1892), Russian poet of German ancestry, associated with the Baltic region and known for his technically exquisite melancholic lyrics on nature and love.

check your breath: exhale, perhaps as when administering a breathalyzer test, but also alluding to the poem's opening.

"I know, the Mongol yoke, the years of famine…"

Blok: Aleksandr Blok (1880–1921), Saint Petersburg Symbolist lyric poet.

land of scoundrels: title of a poem by Sergei Yesenin ("Страна негодяев" 1923).

Chaadaev: Pyotr Chaadaev (1794–1856), Russian philosopher who in his *Philosophical Letters* (*Философские письма* 1826–1831) complained of Russia's intellectual and social-political backwardness and claimed that the nation must develop organically rather than along a Western historical trajectory. He was deemed insane because of his negative views of Russia, a charge he answered in his subsequent "Apologie d'un Fou" (1837).

The Wondrous Raid

Mikhail, Leonid, Yury, Volodyas: likely allusions to Loseff's Leningrad friends and fellow poets: Mikhail Erëmin, Leonid Vinogradov, Yury Mikhailov, Vladimir Ufliand, Vladimir Gerasimov.

Ulyanka, Grazhdanka: suburbs of Leningrad.

Kronstadt: town and seat of the Soviet admiralty, located on an island west of Leningrad, near the head of the Gulf of Finland.

In Memory of Lithuania

hitch up this load of nonsense: the Russian plays on the idiomatic expression "турусы на колёсах," literally "siege towers on wheels," meaning "nonsense."

leaves shits: in the original the first syllables of lines 7 and 8 combine to yield Loseff's original surname.

Kurshes and Prussians: groups of tribes once inhabiting the southern coast of the Baltic Sea, with a culture similar to that of Lithuania. In the twelfth and thirteenth centuries the land was conquered and settled by the Teutonic Knights, and most of the native population was killed. The German name "Prussia" derives from one of these tribes.

"Towards morning I managed to fall asleep…"

To stand on chicken feet: Russian idiom referring to a dilapidated, rickety, tumbledown structure, as a country cottage like that of the fairy-tale character Baba Yaga.

Professor Propp: Vladimir Propp (1895–1970), scholar of linguistics and folklore, renowned for his structuralist interpretations of folklore and fairy-tale motifs in his *The Morphology of the Folktale* (*Морфология сказки* 1928).

This duel is horrible!: quotation from the novel *The Hand; or, The Confession of an Executioner* (*Рука: Повествование палача* 1980), written by Loseff's friend and fellow exile Yuz Aleshkovsky.

Greetings, young, unknown tribe: quotation from Pushkin's poem "Again I visited…" ("Вновь я посетил…" 1835), itself quoted in the first lines of this poem. The salutation, addressed by Pushkin to a grove of young trees that have appeared next to three old pines he used to see a decade ago during his two years in exile, is quoted as well by Joseph Brodsky in his poem "1972" ("1972 год" 1972).

God preserve me…: allusion to Pushkin's poem "God preserve me from losing my mind" ("Не дай мне бог сойти с ума" 1833) and to a sentence from his historical novel *The Captain's Daughter* (*Капитанская дочка* 1836): "God preserve us from seeing a Russian revolt, senseless and merciless" ("Не проведи Бог увидеть русский бунт, бессмысленный и беспощадный").

A Cat's Lament

Wrap me up, O Life…: rhythmical allusion to Nikolai Zabolotsky's poem "Let me have, starling, the little corner/ Lodge me in the old starling-cote" ("Уступи мне, скворец, уголок, / Посели меня в старом скворешнике" 1946).

Departure

the shape of horns: suggests a devil's horns or a cuckold's horns.

The Extended Day

extended day: term for period after normal school day, when children of working parents remain at school until they can be picked up by relatives.

"An extended day for close-cropped heads…"

figs stuffed into pockets: idiom [*фига в кармане*] and practice of expressing concealed resentment or defiance.

"With his timorous wisp of humor…"

Evgeny Shvarts (1896–1958): Soviet dramatist and writer of children's fiction, associated with the "Serapion Brothers" literary group. His play *The Dragon* (Дракон 1944) is a political satire of contemporary Soviet society. The Shvartses and the Lifshitses were friends in Leningrad.

It's good in the theatre, when we aren't there: play on the idiomatic expression *"там хорошо, где нас нет"* ("the grass is always greener on the other side of the fence").

"Above the lake, where one can easily drown…"

The epigraph is from Vasily Zhukovsky's poem "Undine" ("Ундина" 1837).

"I used to work for *Campfire*. In that dreary place…"

Campfire (Костёр): illustrious Soviet magazine for children, where Lev Loseff worked as an editor 1962–1975.

Lotman: Yury Lotman (1922–1993), Soviet literary scholar and cultural historian, famous for his structuralist and semiotic studies of Russian literature and culture.

square circles: literally "fish on fur," itself a play on the expression "fish-lined fur" (*"на рыбьем меху"*), which means shabby clothing.

Morozov: Pavlik Morozov (1918–1932), peasant boy who denounced his father to party authorities for corruption and was lynched; he was celebrated as a martyr in Stalinist propaganda and held up as an ideological exemplar for the Pioneers (Soviet youth movement). "*Moroz*" is Russian for "frost, freezing cold."

chifir: very strong tea possessing narcotic qualities.

"My very best friend and half-enemy…"

Gershenzon: Mikhail O. Gershenzon (1869–1925), philosopher and philologist. The quotation is from his *Wisdom of Pushkin* (*Мудрость Пушкина* 1919).

"While Melpomene and Euterpe…"

zek: Soviet slang for an inmate of a Gulag prison or labor camp.

Alitet Goes to the Hills: novel (*Алитет уходит в горы* 1948) by Tikhon Syomyshkin about the sufferings of the Chukchi people (indigenous to the northeasternmost region of Siberia) at the hands of Americans and kulaks, before they are saved by Bolsheviks; the novel was turned into a popular film in 1949.

chocolates adorned with bears: Soviet "Mishka the Bear" chocolates.

Suvorovesque: Alexandr Vasilievich Suvorov (1729–1800), Russian general famed for never losing a battle, led victorious campaigns against the Ottoman empire (1787–1791), the Polish uprising (1794–1795), and the French in Italy (1799–1800). While he served Empress Catherine with great distinction, he fell out of favor with her son, Paul I, in part because he criticized the new military tactics and modernized uniforms the young emperor had introduced. A statue of Suvorov attired as a young god Mars stands in the Field of Mars in central St. Petersburg.

our bronze creator: allusion to Pushkin's poem "The Bronze Horseman" ("Медный всадник" 1833), referring to a statue of Peter the Great, who founded St. Petersburg. A statue to Pushkin stands in the Mikhailovsky Garden.

Captions to Pictures Seen in Childhood

future saint of Christianity: cf. the stories of St. Eustace and St. Hubertus.

"An onion in bandy slices..."

Ivanov: Aleksandr A. Ivanov (1806–1858), Russian romantic painter.

Shchedrin: Semyon F. Shchedrin (1745–1804), Russian landscape painter.

The Journey
1. In a Park by the Rhine

liszt : a homonym of the Russian "*list*" ("leaf").

meddlesome: original is "*medlennosonnykh*" ("slow-dreaming"), a near-homonym of "Mendelsohn."

"true and tried": original is the inverted archaic phrase "верно и мерно."

sonorous copper: "меди гудящей," an allusion to end of chapter 8 of Nikolai Gogol's tale *Taras Bulba* (*Тарас Бульба* 1835): "And their fame will travel to the ends the entire world, and all who are born later will speak of them: for a mighty word resounds far and wide like the sonorous copper of the bell into which the master craftsman has poured much precious pure silver, so that its beautiful peal may resound afar through cities, hovels, palaces and villages, calling all alike to holy prayer."

2. In an Amsterdam Gallery

Vermeer : an anagram of the Russian "*vremya*" ("time").

3. In the English Channel

Klaipeda: (formerly Memel) Lithuania's major ice-free port and sea-shipping city on the shore of the Baltic.

4. At a Geneva Watchmaker's

cardsharp: Russian "*shuler*," also a homonym of the German "*Schüler*," "schoolboy."

Hey, are you talking about verse?: cf. Paul Valéry's dictum "Rhyme establishes a law independent of the poem's theme and might be compared to a clock outside it" (*Analects*, translated by Stuart Gilbert, [Princeton University Press, 1970], 102).

5. In the Norman Hole

bottle, etched with a fork: original is a pun on "*вилами на воде писано*" ("written on water with a pitchfork"), said of very uncertain predictions.

Life and Fate: (*Жизнь и судьба* 1959; published 1980), epic novel of World War II by Vasily Grossman.

packing up his troubles: original Russian idiom is "to tie up one's grief with a cord," that is, to stop grieving.

drum beats: allusion to Aleksandr Galich's song "Night Patrol" ("Ночной дозор" 1963).

Bakhtin in Saransk

Bakhtin: Mikhail M. Bakhtin (1895–1975), iconoclastic Russian philosopher and literary theorist who achieved international recognition only in the 1960s. A victim of Stalinist purges, he was sentenced to six years internal exile in Kazakhstan, after which in 1936 he moved to Saransk, where he lived for a year teaching courses in the Department of General Literature of the Poleshaev Pedagogical Institute of Mordovia, a teachers' college. In 1945 he returned to Saransk to become chair of the department. The institute was enhanced and renamed the Ogarev University of Mordovia in 1957, and Bakhtin became the chairman of the Department of Russian and Foreign Literature. Deteriorating health forced him to retire in 1961, and in 1969 he and his wife were moved to Moscow, where he could find better medical treatment.

golden-lipped: original "златоуст" from the Greek "*chrusostomos*," meaning an eloquent orator or sermonist; also the name of an early Church Father, John Chrysostom.

Golosovker: Yakov Emmanuilovic Golosovker (1890–1967), Russian philosopher, writer, and translator, known for his scholarly works on myth and logic.

An Interpretation of Tselkov

Tselkov: Oleg Tselkov (b. 1934), Soviet nonconformist artist, expelled from various art institutes for his "formalism." He emigrated to Paris in 1977 and was a close friend of Loseff.

Stanzas

Stanzas: compare poems of the same title by Aleksandr Pushkin (1826), Vladislav Khodasevich (1922), and Anna Akhmatova (1940).

Slightly Stumbling

sacrifice a calf: play on the Russian saying "*заклать упитанного тельца*" ("to sacrifice a fatted calf"), which means "to put on a feast or banquet" (derived from the Biblical story of the prodigal son).

Cloth

the Reaper: original "кондратий" is a folk idiom meaning "apoplectic shock."

the days unravel the rag that You've been given: variation of first line of Joseph Brodsky's poem "The days unravel the rag that You have sewn" ("Дни расплетают тряпочку, сотканную Тобою" 1980).

Lethean library: cf. Vladimir Nabokov, *The Real Life of Sebastian Knight* (1941).

Postcard from New England. 1

poor Evgeny: cf. Aleksandr Pushkin's poem "The Bronze Horseman" ("Медный всадник" 1833).

Rodion: the first name of Raskolnikov, the main character in Dostoevsky's *Crime and Punishment* (*Преступление и наказание* 1866).

Kholstomer: Tolstoy's famous *skaz* story ("Холстомер" 1886), told from the viewpoint of a horse.

hunch-backed [gorbunovaia] shade of Gorchakov: allusion to Joseph Brodsky's long poem "Gorbunov and Gorchakov" ("Горбунов и Горчаков" 1968), about two inmates in a Soviet psychiatric hospital.

Italian tutors: cf. E. A. Baratynsky's poem, "To my Italian Tutor" ("Дядьке-итальянцу" 1844).

Karl Ivanich: the name of the Tolstoy family's German tutor, as recounted in Lev Tolstoy's novel *Childhood* (*Детство* 1852).

Pnin: cf. Vladimir Nabokov's novella, *Pnin* (1957).

to dip his Adidases once again into the same water: cf. Vladimir Nabokov's poem "Refugees" ("Беженцы" 1921).

Arina: Arina Rodionovna, Pushkin's doting nanny, who warmed his spirits during his exile in Mikhailovskoye (1824–1826); cf. his poems "Winter Evening" ("Зимний вечер" 1825), "… again I visited" ("…вновь я посетил" 1835), and "To my Nanny" ("Няне" 1826), echoes of which occur here.

I've raised up a monument: cf. Aleksandr Pushkin's Horatian poem "Exegi monumentum" (1836).

[Liza] Drozdova, Varvara Petrovna: characters in Dostoevsky's novel *The Demons* (*Бесы* 1871–72; also translated as *The Possessed*).

Verses on the Novel

(when the old parents / arrive at the graveyard by the river): allusion to conclusion of Ivan Turgenev's novel *Fathers and Sons* (*Отцы и дети* 1862).

elder (старец): allusion to the monk Father Zosima in Dostoevsky's *Brothers Karamazov* (*Братья Карамазовы* 1880).

Agasha, Sasha: names of minor characters in several of Dostoevsky's novels.

schema: highest monastic degree in the Orthodox Church, the holders of which are bound to observe strict monastic rules.

Karl Ivanich: fictionalized name of the Tolstoy family's German tutor, as recounted in Lev Tolstoy's *Childhood* (*Детство* 1852).

since you don't have a thing: the Russian original plays on the idiom "ни кола ни двора" ("has neither house nor home").

Nicolas: allusion to an episode recounted in Tolstoy's *Youth* (*Юность* 1857), when Sonia Valakhina, the subject of the young author's infatuation, greets him in English after travelling abroad.

gemuetesy: the original "*гемютно*" is a pun on the German word "*gemütlich*."

PBG

Land of Scoundrels: poem by Sergei Yesenin ("Страна негодяев" 1923).

Shestov: Lev Shestov (1866–1938), Russian-Ukrainian existentialist philosopher who strongly influenced Silver Age writers and poets.

Berdyaev: Nikolai Berdyaev (1874–1948), Russian Christian existentialist and political philosopher, exiled to Paris in 1923.

Rozanov: Vasily Rozanov (1856–1919), philosophical essayist who attempted to reconcile Christianity with human sensuality and sexuality; often the adversary of Berdyaev.

Gershenzon: Mikhail Gershenzon (1869–1925), scholar, essayist, and consecutive editor of several influential Russian literary and political journals in the early twentieth century.

Bulgakov: Sergei Bulgakov (1871–1944), Russian Orthodox Christian theologian, philosopher, and economist, exiled to Paris in 1923 along with Berdyaev and other intellectuals. His theological views, influenced by the teaching of Vladimir Solovyov, resulted in his being accused of heresy.

Vyacheslav: Vyacheslav Ivanov (1866–1949), Russian Symbolist poet and essayist, adherent of Nietzsche's theory of Dionysian art, whose weekly salon in Saint Petersburg attracted and influenced the Symbolist poets of the day.

Blok: Aleksandr Blok (1880–1921), Saint Petersburg Symbolist lyric poet.

Katya: character in Blok's poem "The Twelve" ("Двенадцать" 1918).

Kuzmin: Mikhail Kuzmin (1872–1936), Saint Petersburg Symbolist poet and musician.

Burliuk: David Burliuk (1882–1967), Russian poet and painter, one of the founders of Futurism.

Akhmatova: Anna Akhmatova (1889–1966), Russian Acmeist lyric poet.

Speech ("Речь"): daily political, economic, and literary newspaper, published in St. Petersburg 1906–1917.

SR: A member of the Socialist Revolutionary Party. The party was founded in 1902 and played a major role in the organization of the soviets after the 1917 revolution, but thereafter splintered between the Mensheviks and the Bolsheviks and was eventually eclipsed by the latter.

Mandel'shtam: Osip Mandel'shtam (1891–1938), Russian Acmeist poet and essayist. According to Georgii Ivanov, shortly after the Revolution, when Bolsheviks and the Left SR were cooperating, Mandel'shtam went to a café where he could obtain his beloved sweets and found a Left SR, Yakov Bliumkin, drunkenly filling in names on blank death warrants already signed by Felix Dzershinksky (head of the Cheka). Mandel'shtam snatched the warrants from Bliumkin's hands, ripped them up, and ran from the café. See Clarence Brown, *The Prose of Osip Mandelstam* (Princeton: Princeton University Press, 1965), 49–51.

Pushkin Historical Sites

Pushkin: Aleksandr Pushkin (1799–1837), Russia's most venerated poet, who was exiled by the czar to Mikhailovskoye (1824–1826), itself subsequently named a historical site in Pushkin's honor.

dressing, undressing… secret trysts: cf. Pushkin's *Eugene Onegin* (*Евгений Онегин* 1825–1832), 1, XXIII and XI, respectively. Pushkin's "novel in verse" was partly written at Mikhailovskoye.

à la gitane: Pushkin completed his narrative poem "The Gypsies" ("Цыганы" 1824) in Mikhailovskoye.

my decrepit darling nanny: cf. Pushkin's poem "To my Nanny" ("Няне" 1826), who accompanied the poet to Mikhailovskoye.

wondrous moment: cf. Pushkin's poem "To ---" ("К ***" 1825).

Classical

Tan'ka: pun on the Russian idiom *"валять ваньку"* ("to play the fool, play dumb").

Documentary

chicken legs: a ramshackle cottage (*избушка на курьих ножках*).

Olsztyn: a city in northeastern Poland, briefly occupied by Russian forces in 1914 led by Aleksandr Samsonov (1859–1914). German forces led by von Hindenburg eventually encircled and destroyed most of Samsonov's Second Army in what became known as the Battle of Tannenberg. Rather than returning to Russia and Tsar Nicholas II, Samsonov committed suicide on August 29, 1914. Samsonov is also depicted in Aleksandr Solzhenitsyn's *August 1914* (*Август четырнадцатого* 1971).

Instructions to a Heraldic Illustrator

moose, lion: puns on the poet's name: Russian *lev* ("lion") and *los'* ("moose").

Lifshits: the poet's original, given surname before he adopted his pseudonym.

Aesopian tongue: allusion to Loseff's 1984 academic study *On the Beneficence of Censorship: Aesopian Language in Modern Russian Literature*.

"With the rising of the sun we observe..."

early bird...sweet bird: pun on the idiomatic saying "laugh before breakfast and you'll cry before supper" (*"Рано пташечка запела, как бы кошечка не съела,"* literally "the bird sang early, lest the cat eat him up").

"Midway in the journey of my earthly life..."

Midway in the journey: the Russian quotes the first line of Mikhail Lozinsky's translation of Dante's *Divine Comedy*, which won the Stalin Prize in 1946.

an axe suspended in midair: pun on an idiomatic expression for stuffy air (cf. English "so thick you could cut it with a knife").

Muscovites

the old man: Viktor Ardov (1900–1976), writer of satires, literary gossip, and reminiscences, contributor to the popular satirical cartoon magazine *Crocodile* (*Крокодил*).

Anna Andreevna: the poet Anna Akhmatova.

Avvakumian: Avvakum Petrov (1621–1682), priest in the Church of Russia who opposed liturgical reforms instituted by Patriarch Nikon. Avvakum was exiled to the Russian Far East, about which he wrote in his acclaimed *The Life of Archpriest Avvakum by Himself* (*Житие* 1672–1675).

swallowing foolishness: pun on "*выбросить дурь из головы*" ("to get this nonsense out of one's head").

devil in the chair: possible allusion to Lev Tolstoy's story "The Devil" (*Дьявол* 1890, unfinished), the plot of which he considered so scandalous that he hid the manuscript from his wife in the upholstery of a chair in his office.

Tula: Russian city south of Moscow, close to Yasnaia Poliana, Lev Tolstoy's estate.

Amphibronchic Night

1. Evening Paper

Andropov: Yuri Andropov (1914–1984), Soviet politician and, following the death of Leonid Brezhnev, general secretary of the Communist Party of the Soviet Union from November 1982 until his death 15 months later.

2. An Old Dream

Some number tram…thurdy: allusion to Arkadii Severny's song "Tram Number Ten" ("Шёл трамвай десятый номер" 1975) and a popular children's counting rhyme (читалка) "шёл трамвай десятый номер…"

dozen timid: original is a pun on the idiom "not the timid type" ("*не робкого десятка*").

3. Ante Lucem

my heart flew out of my rib cage: allusion to Mikhail Lermontov's poem "If I hear your voice…" ("Слышу ли голос твой" 1838).

Conversation

gloom-and-doomer… last romantic: allusions to popular characterizations of Joseph Brodsky as a romantic poet who draws on classical antiquity.

Lubyanka, Butyrka: prisons in Moscow.

Solovyovka: "little nightingale," but also a diminutive of Vladimir S. Solovyov's name (1853–1900), Russian religious philosopher, critic, and poet. In works including *Lectures on Godmanhood* (Чтения о богочеловенчестве 1878) and *Three Encounters* (Три разговора 1900), he describes his personal experiences with a divine entity he calls "Sophia."

white top: Soviet brand of vodka (with a silver cap).

Liberty: Radio Liberty (along with Radio Free Europe), Western news organization that broadcasts into nondemocratic countries.

Letter to the Old Country

Kuzmin, "Settlers": the quotation is inexact, from Mikhail Kuzmin's 1926 poem in free verse, recounting the depredations of English settlers in America.

vatnik: cotton quilted jacket, often homemade.

"And yet these dreams are beautiful…"

without right to correspondence: Gulag terminology, usually suggesting that the prisoner had been executed.

At Christmas

split in two the star: Loseff comments in an interview that "as is well known, at the moment of the birth of Christ there occurred the rare joint appearance of two planets—Saturn and Jupiter—that appeared from Earth as one new star. In general this is one of the atheistic explanations of evangelical phenomena." "Poet est' peregnoi," Vitali Amurskii (ed.), *Zapechatlennie golosa: Parizhskie besedy s russkimi pisatel'mi i poetami* (Moscow: "MIK," 1998), 71.

"And finally, the bus stop 'Cemetery'..."

Mister Twister: cf. eponymous satirical poem by Samuil Marshak (1933).

no matter what: original is idiomatic, literally "within canon range."

The Tram

Obvodny canal: cf. the poem "Обводный канал" (1928) by Nikolai Zabolotsky. Loseff lived near the Obvodny canal from the late 1940s to the early 1960s.

A March

go I don't know where and get I don't know what: formulaic expression from Russian folk tales.

didn't lose my head: the original plays on the idiomatic expression "*не сносить головы кому*" ("his head will roll, he'll pay for it"), literally "he'll not come back with his head."

No-one (Никто): character from Russian folk tales.

Aleksandr Aleksandrovich Basargin: perhaps a combination of two Decembrists: Aleksandr Aleksandrovich Bestuzhev (1797–1837) and Nikolai Vasil'evich Basargin, the latter of whom was a lieutenant in the Yegerskii Life Guards regiment in St. Petersburg.

Photography Lesson. 1

Compare Vladislav Khodasevich's poems "Before the Mirror" ("Перед зеркалом" 1924) and "Sorrento Photographs" ("Соррентинские фотографии" 1926).

"All the threads have come undone…"

Udel'naia: metro station in Leningrad.

In the Hotel

abominably desolate: allusion to Daniel 9:27.

Dream

kindling (*растопчина*): paronomastic allusion to Countess Evdokiia Rostopchina (1811–1858), Russian poet whose literary salon welcomed poets such as Pushkin, Lermontov, Zhukovsky, and Tyutchev.

bigwig (*шишков*): Admiral Aleksandr Shishkov (1754–1841), a conservative (proto-Slavophile) statesman who wanted all foreign influences on the Russian language removed and was the chief opponent to Nikolai Karamzin's attempts to modernize Russia.

fluffer (*пушков*): character in Daniil Kharms' text "Lecture" ("Лекция" 1940).

pawnish (*пешкин*): Aleksei Maksimovich Peshkov, the actual name of the writer Maksim Gorkii (1868–1936). The two names also yield an anagram of "Pushkin."

"I did not hasten sleep, it happened at once…"

no and *far away*: allusion to a line from chapter VIII of Pushkin's *Eugene Onegin* (*Евгений Онегин* 1825–1832): "some are no more, and others are far away" ("*Иных уж нет, а те далече*").

ne-gative: perhaps pun on Russian "*gad*" (*гад*, slang for "repulsive person").

Pronouns

Compare Boris Pasternak's poem "In Hospital" ("В больнице" 1956)

"The house is filled with warmth ..."

"A Feast in Time of Plague": there is rapture: one of Pushkin's *Little Tragedies* (Маленькие трагедии 1830), a stanza of which reads:

Есть упоение в бою,	There is rapture in a battle,
И бездны мрачной на краю,	And on the brink of the gloomy abyss,
И в разъяренном океане,	And in the furious ocean,
Средь грозных волн и бурной тьмы,	Amid terrible waves and stormy darkness,
И в аравийском урагане,	And in the Arabian whirlwind,
И в дуновении Чумы.	And in the breeze that bears the Plague.

One Day in the Life of Lev Vladimirovich

One Day: cf. Aleksandr Solzhenitsyn's *One Day in the Life of Ivan Denisovich* (Один день Ивана Денисовича 1962).

Northern Palmyra: poetic name for St. Petersburg.

New Holland: island created in 1720 by the canal system in St. Petersburg.

bread of exile: cf. the lyric "The stale bread of exile is hard and bitter" ("Суров и горек черствый хлеб изгнанья" 1829) by the Decembrist poet Wilhelm Küchelbecker.

Baratynsky: Yevgeny Baratynsky (1800–1844), heralded during his lifetime by Pushkin as Russia's finest elegiac poet; after decades of neglect, he was rediscovered by Anna Akhmatova and Joseph Brodsky. Having become disappointed with Moscow salon life, Baratynsky travelled with his family to Paris, eventually to Marseilles, and finally to Naples, where he died.

weaving words: medieval literary technique, now an idiom "плетение словес" meaning a pretentious, vapid style of speaking or writing.

He got his just deserts, he just deserted: a play on the proverb "по Сеньке шапка," which means "to serve someone right."

barin i rab: Russian palindrome, "master and slave."

Mink Brook

Robert Frost: see Frost's poem "West-Running Brook" (1928). The Loseffs lived in a house above an actual west-flowing Mink Brook in New Hampshire.

a grievous feat: the Russian "*с горем пополам*" (literally "halved with grief") means to just barely manage (to do something).

Frost the Red-Nosed: multilingual pun on Nikolai Nekrasov's poem "Frost the Red-Nosed" ("Мороз, красный нос" 1863).

My Book

Lethean Library: cf. Vladimir Nabokov, *The Real Life of Sebastian Knight* (1941).

coach of life: cf. Aleksandr Pushkin's eponymous poem "Телега Жизни" (1823).

"The Swan of the Sweat of the Thorn of Wounds"

Swan of sweat of thorn of wounds: a well-known kenning in old Norse verse.

Varangian: a people from the Baltic region, who between the ninth and eleventh centuries migrated through what later became Russia, Belarus, and the Ukraine. According to the *Primary Chronicle* (Kiev, ca. 1113), one group of Varangians became the Rus' people.

Lay of the Polovtsian defeat: the Polovtsy (also called the Cumans) and their Russian allies were defeated in 1223 by Genghis Khan in the Battle of Kalka River.

Yermak: Yermak Timofeevich (1532/42–1585), Cossack and Russian folk hero who led forces into Siberia to expand the Russian empire. He was wounded in battle, tried to swim across a river, but drowned due to the weight of his armor.

3 Rubles

Fioravanti: Ridolfo "Aristotele" Fioravanti (ca. 1415–1486), Italian architect and engineer, invited to Russia in 1474 by Tsar Ivan III, where he worked on the reconstruction of the Kremlin and built the Assumption Cathedral (Uspensky Sobor, completed in 1479).

De Profundis

De Profundis: cf. the poem of the same title by Anna Akhmatova (1944).

green wine: vodka.

fish, fish, what will you give me?: allusion to Russian folktale "The Golden Fish," also rendered in verse by Pushkin as the "Fairy Tale about the Fisherman and the Fish" ("Сказка о рыбаке и рыбке" 1833).

"A poet is compost, in him dead words…"

a poet is compost: possibly in response to Anna Akhmatova's famous lines "Oh, if you only knew from what trash / Poems grow, knowing no shame" ("Когда б вы знали, из какого сора / Растут стихи, не ведая стыда") in her cycle "Secrets of the Trade" ("Тайны ремесла" 1936–1960).

dead words: allusion to Nikolai Gumilev's poem "The Word" ("Слово" 1919).

larva: Latin term, designating a vengeful spirit of the dead; it also means a costume mask.

paths of grain: allusion to Vladislav Khodasevich's poem "Paths of Grain" ("Путём зерна" 1917) and his eponymously named collection of verse (1920, revised 1922).

In the Ledger

Tambovsky Wolf: a brand of vodka, but also part of the saying "*тамбовский волк тебе товарищ*" ("a tambovsky wolf is your comrade"), to indicate that the speaker does not consider his interlocutor to be on his level or to be a true comrade.

you could just howl ("хоть вой"): pun on the idiomatic "*хоть волком вой*," "it's enough to make you cry" (literally "howl like a wolf"), said of an intolerable situation.

Chekist: member of the Cheka, the Soviet security police 1918–1922.

Levlosev

citharoede: possibly an allusion to Varro's maxim "non omnes qui habent citharam, sunt citharoedi" ("not all who own lyres are lyre-players").

Marinist: Marina Tsvetaeva (1892–1941), Russian experimental poet.

Velimirician: Velimir Khlebnikov (1885–1922), Russian Futurist poet.

Brodskyite: Josef Brodsky (1940–1996), Russian poet, friend of Loseff's.

Osipologist: Osip Mandelshtam (1891–1938), Russian Acmeist poet.

Annophile: Anna Akhmatova (1889–1966), Russian Acmeist lyric poet.

Aleksandromaniac: Aleksandr Blok (1880–1921), Russian Symbolist poet.

don't hold your breath: the original has the literal meaning of "hold open your pocket" and idiomatic meaning of "not a chance."

heard the ringing... hears the tolling: the Russian is a play on a colloquialism equivalent to "not knowing what one's talking about."

the thatch is reputedly edible: pun on the proverb "дома и солома едома" ("at home even the thatch [roof] is edible"), meaning "there's no place like home."

Twelve Colleges

Twelve Colleges: former Leningrad State University (now University of St. Petersburg), located in buildings originally built by Peter the Great to house the twelve colleges (later ministries) of the government.

I lie: pun on the initials of Leningrad State University (LGU), which is also the first person indicative of the verb "to lie" (tell falsehoods).

stood on a shore of desolate waves/ and gazed into the distance: allusion to the opening lines of Pushkin's poem "The Bronze Horseman" ("Медный всадник" 1833).

Victory: Soviet car make of the 1940s and 1950s.

future Aesopians: self-referentially anticipating Loseff's 1984 academic study *On the Beneficence of Censorship: Aesopian Language in Modern Russian Literature*.

potato fields: mandatory help during harvest for all university students during their vacation. Loseff was caught reading Nietzsche, at the time considered a "fascist" writer.

take someone on a reconnaissance mission: Soviet slang from World War II, meaning "to trust someone."

the hut turned its backside to me: magic formula used in Russian fairy tales.

I got the gate: pun on Russian idiom "*от ворот поворот*" ("to send packing, brush off").

"The raven's corpse began to caw…"

A mirror: A. A. Tarkovsky's film *The Mirror* (Зеркало 1975) was deeply admired by Loseff.

not made by human hands: suggests the first line of Pushkin's poem "Exegi monumentum" (1836): "*Я памятник себе воздвиг нерукотворный.*"

Allegory

Artek: all-union and international Soviet Young Pioneer Camp, located on the Crimean Peninsula.

SPUYTEN DUYVIL
Meeting Eyes Bindery
Triton
Lithic Scatter

8TH AVENUE Stefan Brecht
ABROAD: AN EXPATRIATE'S DIARIES Harriet Sohmers Zwerling
A DAY AND A NIGHT AT THE BATHS Michael Rumaker
ACTS OF LEVITATION Laynie Browne
ALIEN MATTER Regina Derieva
ANARCHY Mark Scroggins
APO/CALYPSO Gordon Osing
APPLES OF THE EARTH Dina Elenbogen
APPROXIMATING DIAPASON j/j hastain & t thilleman
ARC: CLEAVAGE OF GHOSTS Noam Mor
THE ARSENIC LOBSTER Peter Grandbois
ASHES RAIN DOWN William Luvaas
AUNTIE VARVARA'S CLIENTS Stelian Tanase
BALKAN ROULETTE Drazan Gunjaca
THE BANKS OF HUNGER AND HARDSHIP J. Hunter Patterson
BEAUTIFUL SOUL Joshua Corey
BEHIND THE WALL AT THE SUGAR WORKS Marc Vincenz
LA BELLE DAME Gordon Osing & Tom Carlson
BIRD ON THE WING Juana Culhane
BLACK LACE Barbara Henning
BLACK MOUNTAIN DAYS Michael Rumaker
BLUEPRINTS FOR A GENOCIDE Rob Cook
BOTH SIDES OF THE NIGER Andrew Kaufman
BREATHING FREE (ed.) Vyt Bakaitis
BURIAL SHIP Nikki Stiller
BUTTERFLIES Brane Mozetic
BUT THEY, UM Jennie Neighbors
BY THE TIME YOU FINISH THIS BOOK YOU MIGHT BE DEAD Aaron Zimmerman
CADENCES j/j hastain
CAPTIVITY NARRATIVES Richard Blevins
CELESTIAL MONSTER Juana Culhane
CEPHALONICAL SKETCHES t thilleman

CLEF   j/j hastain & t thilleman
CLEOPATRA HAUNTS THE HUDSON   Sarah White
CLOUD FIRE   Katherine Hastings
COLUMNS: TRACK 2   Norman Finkelstein
CONSCIOUSNESS SUITE   David Landrey
THE CONVICTION & SUBSEQUENT
            LIFE OF SAVIOR NECK   Christian TeBordo
CONVICTION'S NET OF BRANCHES   Michael Heller
THE CORYBANTES   Tod Thilleman
CROSSING BORDERS   Kowit & Silverberg
CRYPTO-ARKANSAS   Mark Spitzer
DAY BOOK OF A VIRTUAL POET   Robert Creeley
THE DAY HE'S GONE   Paweł Marcinkiewicz   trans. Piotr Florczyk
DAYLIGHT TO DIRTY WORK   Tod Thilleman
THE DESIRE NOTEBOOKS   John High
DETECTIVE SENTENCES   Barbara Henning
DIARY OF A CLONE   Saviana Stanescu
DIFFIDENCE   Jean Harris
DONNA CAMERON   Donna Cameron
DON'T KILL ANYONE, I LOVE YOU   Gojmir Polajnar
DRAY-KHMARA AS A POET   Oxana Asher
EGGHEAD TO UNDERHOOF   Tod Thilleman
ELSA   Tsipi Keller
EROTICIZING THE NATION   Leverett T. Smith, Jr.
THE EVIL QUEEN   Benjamin Perez
EXILED FROM THE WOMB   Adrian Sangeorzan
EXTREME POSITIONS   Stephen Bett
THE FARCE   Carmen Firan
FISSION AMONG THE FANATICS   Tom Bradley
THE FLAME CHARTS   Paul Oppenheimer
FLYING IN WATER   Barbara Tomash
FORM   Martin Nakell
FOUR SEASONS   Michael Forstrom
GESTURE THROUGH TIME   Elizabeth Block
GHOSTS!   Martine Bellen
GIRAFFES IN HIDING   Carol Novack
GNOSTIC FREQUENCIES   Patrick Pritchett
GOD'S WHISPER   Dennis Barone

GOWANUS CANAL, HANS KNUDSEN   Tod Thilleman
GRAPHOMANIA   j/j hastain
HALF-GIRL   Stephanie Dickinson
HE KNOWS WHAT A STICK IS   Russell Brickey
HIDDEN DEATH, HIDDEN ESCAPE   Liviu Georgescu
HOUNDSTOOTH   David Wirthlin
HOW TO WALK AWAY   Lisa Birman
IDENTITY   Basil King
IN TIMES OF DANGER   Paul Oppenheimer
INCRETION   Brian Strang
INFERNO   Carmen Firan
INFINITY SUBSECTIONS   Mark DuCharme
INSOUCIANCE   Thomas Phillips
IN THAILAND WITH THE APOSTLES   Joanna Sit
INVERTED CURVATURES   Francis Raven
THE IVORY HOUR   Laynie Browne
JACKPOT   Tsipi Keller
THE JAZZER & THE LOITERING LADY   Gordon Osing
KISSING NESTS   Werner Lutz, trans. by Marc Vincenz
KNOWLEDGE   Michael Heller
LADY V.   D.R. Popa
LAST SUPPER OF THE SENSES   Dean Kostos
LAWFULLY WEDDED WIVES   Nona Caspers & Joell Hallowell
A LESSER DAY   Andrea Scrima
LET'S TALK ABOUT DEATH   M. Maurice Abitbol
LIBRETTO FOR THE EXHAUSTED WORLD   Michael Fisher
LIGHT HOUSE   Brian Lucas
LIGHT YEARS: MULTIMEDIA IN THE EAST VILLAGE,
                1960-1966   (ed.) Carol Bergé
LITTLE BOOK OF DAYS   Nona Caspers
LITTLE TALES OF FAMILY & WAR   Martha King
LONG FALL: ESSAYS AND TEXTS   Andrey Gritsman
LUNACIES   Ruxandra Cesereanu
LUST SERIES   Stephanie Dickinson
LYRICAL INTERFERENCE   Norman Finkelstein
MAINE BOOK   Joe Cardarelli (ed.) Anselm Hollo
MANNHATTEN   Sarah Rosenthal
MATING IN CAPTIVITY   Nava Renek

Meanwhile   Gordon Osing
Medieval Ohio   Richard Blevins
Memory's Wake   Derek Owens
Mermaid's Purse   Laynie Browne
Miming Mink   j/j hastain
The Minotaur's Daughter   Rowland Saifi
Mobility Lounge   David Lincoln
Modern Adventures   Bill Evans
The Moscoviad   Yuri Andrukhovych
Multifesto: A Henri d'Mescan Reader
        (remix edition)   Davis Schneiderman
My Last Century   Joanna Sit
The New Beautiful Tendons   Jeffery Beam
Nighthawks   Katherine Hastings
Nightshift / An Area of Shadows   Erika Burkart & Ernst Halter
No Perfect Words   Nava Renek
No Wrong Notes   Norman Weinstein
North & South   Martha King
Notes of a Nude Model   Harriet Sohmers Zwerling
The Number of Missing   Adam Berlin
Of All The Corners To Forget   Gian Lombardo
One Foot Out the Door   Lewis Warsh
Onönyxa & Therseyn   T Thilleman
The Opening Day   Richard Blevins
Our Father   M.G. Stephens
Over the Lifeline   Adrian Sangeorzan
Pagan Days   Michael Rumaker
Part of The Design   Laura E. Wright
Pieces for Small Orchestra & other fictions   Norman Lock
The Pigs Drink From Infinity   Mark Spitzer
A Place in the Sun   Lewis Warsh
The Poet : Pencil Portraits   Basil King
Political Ecosystems   J.P. Harpignies
Powers: Track 3   Norman Finkelstein
The Prison Notebooks of Alan Krieger (Terrorist)   Marc Estrin
The Propaganda Factory   Marc Vincenz

Remains to be Seen   Halvard Johnson
Retelling   Tsipi Keller
Rivering   Dean Kostos
Root-Cellar to Riverine   Tod Thilleman
The Roots of Human Sexuality   M. Maurice Abitbol
Saigon and other poems   Jack Walters
A Sardine on Vacation   Robert Castle
Savoir Fear   Charles Borkhuis
Secret of White   Barbara Tomash
Seduction   Lynda Schor
See What You Think   David Rosenberg
Selected Early Poems of Lev Loseff   (ed.) Henry Pickford
Semi-Sleep   Kenneth Baron
Settlement   Martin Nakell
Sex and the Senior City   M. Maurice Abitbol
Sexual Harassment Rules   Lynda Schor
Shader   Daniel Nester
Sketches in Norse & Forra   t thilleman
Sketches Tzitzimime   t thilleman
Slaughtering the Buddha   Gordon Osing
Snailhorn (fragments)   t thilleman
The Snail's Song   Alta Ifland
SOS: Song of Songs of Solomon   j/j hastain
The Spark Singer   Jade Sylvan
Spiritland   Nava Renek
State of the Union   Susan Lewis
Strange Evolutionary Flowers   Lizbeth Rymland
Suddenly Today We Can Dream   Rutha Rosen
The Sudden Death of...   Serge Gavronsky
The Takeaway Bin   Toni Mirosevich
The Tattered Lion   Juana Culhane
Tautological Eye   Martin Nakell
Ted's Favorite Skirt   Lewis Warsh
Theaters of Skin   Gordon Osing & Tom Carlson
Things That Never Happened   Gordon Osing
Thread   Vasyl Makhno

THREE MOUTHS   Tod Thilleman
THREE SEA MONSTERS   Tod Thilleman
TO KILL A CARDINAL   Michael Rumaker
THE TOMMY PLANS   Cooper Renner
TRACK   Norman Finkelstein
TRANSITORY   Jane Augustine
TRANSPARENCIES LIFTED FROM NOON   Chris Glomski
TRIPLE CROWN SONNETS   Jeffrey Cyphers Wright
TSIM-TSUM   Marc Estrin
TWELVE CIRCLES   Yuri Andrukhovych
VIENNA ØØ   Eugene K. Garber
UNCENSORED SONGS FOR SAM ABRAMS   (ed.) John Roche
UP FISH CREEK ROAD   David Matlin
VENICE IS FOR CATS   Nava Renek & Ethel Renek
WARP SPASM   Basil King
WATCHFULNESS   Peter O'Leary
WATCH THE DOORS AS THEY CLOSE   Karen Lillis
WALKING AFTER MIDNIGHT   Bill Kushner
WEST OF WEST END   Peter Freund
WHEN THE GODS COME HOME TO ROOST   Marc Estrin
WHIRLIGIG   Christopher Salerno
WHITE, CHRISTIAN   Christopher Stoddard
WINTER LETTERS   Vasyl Makhno
WITHIN THE SPACE BETWEEN   Stacy Cartledge
A WORLD OF NOTHING BUT NATIONS   Tod Thilleman
A WORLD OF NOTHING BUT SELF-INFLICTION   Tod Thilleman
WANDERING ON COURSE   Robert Podgurski
WRECKAGE OF REASON   (ed.) Nava Renek
WRECKAGE OF REASON 2 :
    BACK TO THE DRAWING BOARD   (ed.) Nava Renek
XIAN DYAD   Jason Price Everett
THE YELLOW HOUSE   Robin Behn
YOU, ME, AND THE INSECTS   Barbara Henning

www.ingramcontent.com/pod-product-compliance
Lightning Source LLC
Chambersburg PA
CBHW060509300426
44112CB00017B/2597